The Book of Margins

D1546252

Religion and Postmodernism
A series edited by Mark C. Taylor

The Book of Margins

Edmond Jabès

Translated by
Rosmarie Waldrop
With a Foreword by Mark C. Taylor

The University of Chicago Press
Chicago and London

Edmond Jabès was born in Cairo in 1912 and lived in France from 1956 until his death in 1991. His work, translated throughout the world, has received numerous honors, including the Prix des Critiques, the Prize for Arts, Letters, and Science of the Foundation for French Judaism, the Grand Prix National de Poésie, the Pasolini Prize, and the Cittadella Prize. **Rosmarie Waldrop,** a poet and editor/publisher of Burning Deck Press, is also the English translator of Jabès's *The Book of Questions* and *The Book of Shares.*

Published as *Le livre des marges* by Fata Morgana (the first part was originally published in 1975 as *Ça suit son cours,* and the second part in 1984 as *Dans la double dépendance du dit*); © Editions Fata Morgana 1975, 1984.

The University of Chicago Press, Chicago 60637
The University of Chicago Press, Ltd., London
© 1993 by The University of Chicago
All rights reserved. Published 1993
Printed in the United States of America

02 01 00 99 98 97 96 95 94 93   1 2 3 4 5

ISBN: 0-226-38888-3 (cloth)
      0-226-38889-1 (paper)

Library of Congress Cataloging-in-Publication Data

Jabès, Edmond.
    [Livre des marges. English]
    The book of margins / Edmond Jabès ; translated by
Rosmarie Waldrop ; with a foreword by Mark C. Taylor.
        p.   cm. — (Religion and postmodernism)
    I. Series.
    PQ2619.A112L4813   1993
    848'.91407—dc20   92-31405
                                                CIP

⊗ The paper used in this publication meets the minimum
requirements of the American National Standard for
Information Sciences—Permanence of Paper for Printed
Library Materials, ANSI Z39.48-1984.

Contents

1
It Goes Its Way

2
Doubly Dependent on the Said

Series Editor's Foreword

It was nearly a decade ago when I first met Edmond Jabès. Though long impressed by the haunting portrait on the jackets of most of his books, I was not prepared for the power of his face. Lines too deep to be read and eyes whose piercing blue remained unfathomable created a text beyond decipherment. We talked most of the afternoon—sometimes in French, sometimes in English. While much was lost in translation, I quickly realized that the problem of language was not merely the result of our mutual difficulties in a foreign tongue. In the halts and pauses of our conversation, something else, something other was stirring. It was precisely this unnameable other that initially had drawn me to Jabès's writings and had brought me to rue Epée de Bois.

Things did not begin well. In my faltering French, I made the mistake of referring to him as "a Jewish writer." Obviously irritated, he abruptly interrupted me: "I am *not* a Jewish writer; I am a writer and a Jew." The distinction, at first obscure, gradually became somewhat clearer.

"I came to Judaism through an interrogation of the book."

"Why the book?" I asked.

"Though I did not practice the faith, I had to leave Egypt because I was a Jew. It seemed that my destiny was tied to the book in complex ways that I felt obligated to try to understand. As I probed more deeply, I began to realize that Judaism is an extended lesson in reading, which involves an endless questioning of the writer. Adorno once said that after

Auschwitz we can no longer write poetry. I say that after Auschwitz we *must* write poetry but with wounded words." In his brief reply, Jabès provided the coordinates that orient his work: writing, reading, and the book—all inscribed in wounded words. The book whose writing and reading obsess Jabès is never closed but is a book of questions that remains forever unfinished. Questioning is not simply a writerly pose but is an inescapable condition.

> The question means that, for the time of its formulation, we do not belong. We do not belong with belonging; we are unbound within bonds. Detached, in order to become more fully attached and then again detached. It means we forever turn the *inside out,* set it free, revel in its freedom and die of it.

The time of the formulation of the question never ends, for it is always the questioner who is in question. The endlessness of the question means that we never belong anywhere or always belong to unbelonging. Exile from Egypt—or elsewhere—is neither accidental nor passing but is as unavoidable and chronic as time itself.

Exile, however, is not only, indeed is not primarily, a matter of spatial and temporal dislocation. For Jabès, the topos of exile is writing. Writing at once interrogates and enacts the condition of unbelonging from which there is no escape. In a certain sense, Jabès's texts recount stories that are not stories and events that are not events. They tell us *nothing.*

A sound—uttered by whom?—and then nothing.
A word—written by whom?—and then a blank.
Listen to the nothing. Read the blank.

To read Jabès patiently and thoughtfully—he can be read in no other way—is to listen to nothing by reading the blank.

Like the gaps in our exchange, the blanks that rend Jabès's text fall in the pauses and spaces that punctuate his seemingly incessant conversations. His writings are never monological but are always dialogues and dialogues within dialogues—dialogues among imaginary characters, dialogues with other writers living and dead, and, most important, dialogues with an other who is never named. Books open onto other books, making it difficult to know where one work ends and another begins. Texts appropriate but do not cite other texts—some by Jabès, some by others—throwing the identity of the author into question. As the boundaries among and within texts ceaselessly proliferate and shift, every book becomes a book of margins.

The Book of Margins, however, occupies a unique place in Jabès's oeuvre. Describing this work, he explains:

> The texts gathered here are meant to stay in the margins of my work. We must leave them their marginal character, even emphasize it, for a freer reading. They owe nothing to the All but, on the contrary, owe all to Nothing. Hence their unquenched desire for All and their primal fear of Nothing.
>
> I would like them to be received as writing of the vertigo where book opens to book.

Rather than an integrated whole, *The Book of Margins* is a heterogeneous collage of texts. Most of the so-called book extends Jabès's characteristic style, which is neither precisely prose nor poetry, but a third genre which, though difficult to define, is unmistakable. Jabès's meditation is suspended between opposites he can neither escape nor reconcile: presence/absence, life/death, fullness/emptiness, light/darkness, white/black, proximity/distance, visible/invisible, conditioned/unconditioned, thought/unthought, disclosure/concealment, saying/unsayable, and writing/silence. Above all, writing/silence.

Unlike other works, the quasi-poetry of *The Book of Margins* is interrupted by discursive sections in which Jabès directly engages many of the writers who are usually silent partners in his dialogues: Paul Celan, René Char, Roger Caillois, Max Jacob, Gabriel Bounoure, Jean Grenier, P. P. Pasolini, Louis-René des Forêts, Michel Leiris, Georges Bataille, Emmanuel Lévinas, Maurice Blanchot, and Jacques Derrida. Jabès's comments on many of the writers who have set the terms of contemporary critical debate lend *The Book of Margins* its special significance. Though his remarks are brief and often elliptical, Jabès's careful readings of others suggest that the intertextual weave he fabricates extends far beyond the limits of "his own" works. As book opens to book, the margins of writing fold and refold to produce a text that approaches infinity.

The approach of infinity marks yet another margin, a different margin that plays along the margins of Jabès's text.

Wide, the margin between *carte blanche* and white page. Nevertheless it is not in this margin that you can find me, but in the yet whiter one that separates the word-strewn sheet from the transparent, the written page from the one to be written: In the infinite space where the eye turns back to the eye, and the hand to the pen, where all we write is erased even as we write it. For the book imperceptibly takes shape within the book we will never finish.

There is my desert.

The whiter margin, which is the invisible site of the book yet to be written, is the space or spacing of the absence of the book. This absence is no simple absence; the absence of the book is the no-place where an infinite withdrawal allows appearances to appear. It is precisely this withdrawing absence that summons Jabès to write and us to read. Exploring "the absence of the book," Blanchot remarks:

> The attraction of (pure) exteriority or the vertigo of space as distance, fragmentation that only drives us back to the fragmentary.
>
> The absence of the book: the prior deterioration of the book, the game of dissidence it plays with reference to the space in which it is inscribed; the preliminary dying of the book. Writing, the relation to every book's *other*, to what is de-scription in the book, a scriptuary demand beyond discourse, beyond language. The act of writing at the edge of the book, outside the book.

To write *sensu strictissimo* is always to write at the edge of the book in what can never be anything other than a book of margins. The margin is the liminal space separating the written page from the page that always remains to be written. The scriptuary demand to which the book is a response comes from elsewhere, in the name of another who is never named or is named only improperly. For Jabès, one of the pseudonyms of the unnameable Other is "God." God never speaks directly but only approaches indirectly in the faults of language and silence of words.

> God's truth is in silence.
> To fall silent in turn, with the
> hope of dissolving into it.
> But we become aware of it only
> through words.
> And words, alas, drive us ever far-
> ther from our goal.

The one who attempts to break the silence of truth by writing the truth of silence faces a double bind: silence can be heard only in and through the words that destroy it. Silence, in other words, fades in its very uttering. The disappearance of silence clears the space in which language is articulated. In struggling to form language from silence, the writer reenacts a drama that is as old as creation itself.

Though Jabès rarely comments on the sources of his reflection, his writing is, in effect, a scriptural repetition of the Kabbalistic interpretation of creation. Like the ever elusive *tsimtsum*, silence is the white space whose withdrawal marks the emergence of the black space of the created wor(l)d. When read in this way, the point of writing is the writing of the point. Jabès begins the last volume of *The Book of Questions, El, or The Book*, with two lines from the Kabbalah.

When God, *El,* wanted to reveal Himself
He appeared as a point.

Such a revelation is, of course, a concealment, for the point
does really not exist. Like the silence that echoes it, the point
can only appear by disappearing.
    The point is not . . . that God is silent . . . but that God is
silence itself.

          Four times God fell silent in His Name. Four
          times, on the way up and down each slope of the
          mountain, have we faced the silence of the letter.

          "Pride is the hope to conquer the four divine let-
          ters of the unpronounceable Name, and our fall, to
          be inevitably engulfed in each one," she said.

The color of silence is white. The margins of *The Book of
Margins* are the white space where silence speaks. To hear
silence truly—if, indeed, it can be heard—it is not enough to
become silent. Rather, one must become silence.

          To fall silent in turn, with the
          hope of dissolving into it.

          *

If exile is neither accidental nor passing but is as unavoidable and chronic as time itself, then the place of our erring is
a desert we can never escape. Jabès quotes Gabriel Bounoure,
who is commenting on Jabès:

The desert, by its exclusion of housing, opens an infinite elsewhere to man's essential erring. Here, no here makes sense. And when a human voice rises in this non-environment, Presence and Absence battle at the core of its every word, with Absence winning out.

After we had talked for several hours, we approached a point—perhaps the point—that seemed to preoccupy Jabès. Rising in his chair, he became agitated and spoke with an intensity I have rarely heard: "It is very hard to live with silence. The real silence is death and this is terrible. To approach this silence, it is necessary to journey into the desert. You do not go to the desert to find identity, but to lose it, to lose your personality, to become anonymous. You make yourself void. You *become* silence. You must become more silent than the silence around you. And then something extraordinary happens: you hear silence speak."

Listen . . . listen carefully . . . listen patiently to the silence of Jabès's writing. In his wounded words, something Other stirs. Whether we name this other "God" or insist on different names for the unnameable, we gradually realize that altarity interrogates us endlessly.

*

P.S. It is not life that creates, but death.

And now only ashes remain.

Ashes
　　Ashes
Ashes
Remain
Remains
　　Of what doesn't
Remain

There is no memorial—how could there be for one who devoted his life to the immemorial? Simply a plaque bearing the
inscription:

Edmond Jabès
Ecrivain

In a certain sense, he had always been writing from the grave.
As his body turns to ash—black ash, his words turn to
sand—white sand. Jabès concludes his "Farewell" in *The
Book of Questions* by borrowing words from Robert Gilbert-
Lecomte: "The wind of the spirit blows only in the desert."
Abandoning us to find spirit in the desert of his texts, Edmond
Jabès has finally become the silence his wounded words could
never break.

Mark C. Taylor
Williamstown

1

It Goes Its Way

for Maurice Nadeau

"Can it be that, in the book, dying means becoming invisible to all others, but decipherable to yourself?"

(Aely)

"Could it be that, in the book, writing means becoming legible to all others, but undecipherable to yourself?"

". . . for *dying* is a manner of seeing the invisible . . ."

Maurice Blanchot
("Discours sur la patience,"
Le Nouveau Commerce,
Spring 1975)

If my freedom were not in the book, where would it be?

If my book were not my freedom, what would it be?

Truth cannot but be violent. There is no peaceable truth.

All violence is part of day.

Death, which is the end of day, is also violence come to its end.

The *involuntary* has always, for us, been the *inevitable*.

Tomorrow remains forever open to tomorrow; truth, to truth; day to day; night, to night; violence, to infinite violence.

The violence of the book is turned against the book: battle without mercy.

Writing means perhaps taking on, in the word, the unforeseeable phases of this combat, where God, unsuspected hoard of aggressive force, is the unmentionable stake.

Page without Date, Undatable

Death's shadow is white.

I

THE POWER TO NAME

The time of the writer is a function of the life of the sign, of inspiration or expiration governed by that of the book—of, as it were, an absence of time maintained within time by the word's own time, hence of an immeasurable time as opposed to that of our timepieces.

It is in this other time, at time's edge, that I find you again, dear Gabriel Bounoure. The infinite suits you. The infinite where your feet carried you and one evening forsook you, and which now alone has the power to name you.

II

AT THE FOOT OF THE PAGE

(My friends know how withdrawn a life I live; not that I have an excessive cult of solitude, but writing always isolates the person who undertakes it and chains him where he hoped to be set free.)

"Death means reading."

(Yaël)

"Only the reader is real."

(Je bâtis ma demeure)

"How many times did I think I was saved when in fact I was drowning," he said.

III

READING

The writer can get free of his writing only by using it, that is, by reading himself. As if the aim of writing were to use what is already written as a launching pad for reading the writing to come.

Moreover, what he has written is read in the process, hence constantly modified by his reading.

The book comes into being by allowing itself to be read as it will be. The written word initiates reading; this is its immediate difference from the spoken word. The *written* replaces the spoken, not the better to fix or formulate it, but, on the contrary, to enjoy its explosion as each part is exposed to reading at its various stages, its different levels of sense.

It is the eye, not the ear, that launches the true questioning, the interrogation of the thousand questions that lie dormant in each letter.

Reading is master of the sign. But is it not of and in the sign that reading is born and dies, that a glance is born and buried?

"A bad book is perhaps simply a book badly read by its author," he said.

> (. . . *because there is nothing but menaced traces, embryos of discourse, once the book has been articulated and the unstoppable word given free rein—the book being made against the grain of the book, hence simultaneously unmaking itself to remain book-in-process; word separating from word to die after in its assigned place. This is because all that is graspable is no sooner grasped than it escapes this bondage and gradually ties into a network of contradictory relations which, if they reduce it to its function as sign, image, sound, as sign among signs, image among images, sound among sounds, nevertheless also free it from the oppressive yoke of sense, the tyranny of Totality. As if it had to become Nothing's All in order not to be All's Nothing.)*

*

The book is an unbearable totality. I write against a background of facets.

Writing puts us into words to make us part of its movement. Then no one can help us.

God, rebel name of the abyss.

For man, for the object, an acceptable name. For the invisible, a name that cannot be pronounced.

(Visibility of the invisible!
To think of God as apotheosis of the neutral,
dwindling reality, radiant irreality.)

*

Being partisan or opponent to a particular work is, a priori, suspect. We admire or condemn what we retain of a work, that is, what we have drawn from it and made our own. Hence the immense liberties any reader takes with a book. But the book never belongs to one person alone. It only seems to submit to the reader. Being prey to all possible readings it is, finally, prey to none.

("Where can we find a criterion to distinguish
true work from mere stuttering? There is no crite-
rion but reading and rereading—no criterion but
long acquaintance—to help us discover what in a
work links its deep origin to an affirmation of last-
ing, stirring presence."
Gabriel Bounoure
(Preface to *Marelles sur le Parvis*)

Literary history is, in some way, a paltry history of mere vengeance. Now the book, carried by the enthusiasm of a few, triumphs over ignorance or manifest hostility; now the reader, turning to new and closer works, wipes out a sometimes burdensome past.

So time goes by, read, written; reread, rewritten.

One day, the writer is confronted with the commentaries his work has inspired. He suddenly feels at the mercy of countless spotlights focused on him wherever he goes, wherever he takes refuge. These spotlights track with indifference the course of his glory or misery.

Of these I shall not talk in this book.

*

How could we fail to see that neutrality, with its long and frequent divagations from the unknown to the more familiar, is determined to stand aside prudently, in legitimate fear of being taken for what it must all too soon become: *the key to reality.*

The stars' indifference toward the space that houses them is comparable to that of the night which allows them to glitter.

This reciprocal indifference fed by the infinite is, in both its negation and affirmation, the distance distanced by neutrality.

God, who is the indifference of all distance, is the blind insolence of the neutral.

Higher than the highest, lower than the lowest, the neutral.

No neutrality for irresolute reflections.
Half-light means non-existence.

O key on a solid ring of space, with teeth of the unknown, with casings of the infinite. . .

An existence within non-existence: like a knife.
Neutrality cuts.

Neutrality of place: air, paper, marble.

Letters, syllables, words in the end all give way
to the neutral space they had in part tried to occupy.

To think of God, the Place of places, as excess
neutrality.

The sign is mounted on the neutral. Hence it is a
sign of the neutral, as the grain of sand is a sheen of
the infinite.

The unreality of the real is sometimes the unwar-
ranted reality of the neutral.

Key to the book: neutrality, the real light.

Every page turned in a book is a door closing
behind us, a door that has forgotten its name.

The neutral is the extreme daring of the name, its
freedom set free.

The key to the book is the key to the name.

Our ties work through what sets us free: a thirst
for neutrality.

Who can tell the warmth of a grain of sand or its
coolness at night? This is, daily, the temperature
range of the neutral.

Cold at the heart of cold, burning in front of the fire, the neutral survives second by second.

To go for the neutral, to touch center, to mark the boundary point.

Milieu: *mille lieux,* a thousand places.

All and Nothing are the two poles of the neutral.

"For the nomad, space avoids itself. It becomes a void place, whose undifferentiated parts join point-lessly together."

Gabriel Bounoure
("E.J. ou la guérison par le livre,"
Lettres Nouvelles,
July–September 1966)

Neutrality: way of the void, voided by the same token.

—No road in the desert, but now and then a derelict footstep.

From one night to the next, earth, water, and fire recite the neutrality of the divine.

"To give explanations for the inexplicable."

Gabriel Bounoure
(Preface to *Marelles sur le Parvis*)

"... The desert, by its exclusion of housing, opens an infinite elsewhere to man's essential wandering. Here, no here makes sense. And when a human voice rises in this non-environment, Presence and Absence battle at the core of its every word, with Absence winning out."

Gabriel Bounoure
("E. J. la demeure et le livre,"
Mercure de France, January 1965)

(What can be said is said in what will never be said, for all its being said.

If the text is in cipher, lean on the zeros.

In the timeless attraction of positive for negative, and negative for positive, enter the time of neutrality.

The neutrality of the cipher attests the literalness of the text.)

*

Absence: stubborn heaven of the neutral.

Nothing is impossible for the neutral. At its confines it is the impossible preserved: the line of the horizon.

The unthought remains a walled-up door, blocked passageway, sly death.

Impatient, our thinking. The unthought—what eludes thought and even the question of thought—is perhaps an infinite, passive patience at the edge of the void.

This impersonal weight that is the universe. . .
Weight of the neutral, crushing weight of the last world.
To die means finally to embrace the neutral, to carry it, now lighter, on our shoulders.

Neutral wall of anticipated centuries; so many foreheads touch it in fervor or humility and bleed.

From sense to nonsense, from life to death, from river to sea, wide sandy highways of the neutral.

"The unthought," he said, "is (who knows?) what no longer exists in our thinking—or, rather, only as leaven: an unimaginable thought back before what is before thought."

Does thought return to the unthought as to its origin? Then there is no thinkable origin. Then God is forever lost in God.

Closest to sap: the neutral.

From now on we shall call *neutral* all veer from *null*.

First Step

(The word imposes its sense on the non-sense from which it issued.

The sense of words is that of their adventure, the sense they grant—and make us attribute—to their own unfurling and erasure.

"All I know came to me through the word," he said. "The word reveals, and reveals itself. The writer is without mystery."

Right word. Righteous death.

The world is in a word. Death of a word, death of a world.

To the impossible book the word vows impossible love, with a mixture of joy and fright.

There is no sense to the word, but, rather, a law respected by sense.

"Sense," he said, "would be a simple convention of reading or listening, if the frustrated letters did not have to add their grain of salt.

To each vocable its share of sense, that is, its share of death revealed.

"Writing, O landscape of chasms and crests, is a faithful replica of our conquests and defeats within death. This is why everybody has his own way of writing," he said. "And the voice follows its contour."

One single name for life and death: ours?

God has a name He has taken from ours, a place He made us lose.

"From the way he speaks I can tell if he writes straight or slant, large or small, and at the foot of which mountain he will die," he also said.

To die in peace: to die without words.)

Then thought is perhaps the direction of a glance defied and modified by words.

The course of thought is the illuminating road of death.

Vast night of the book. Stars spell the words.

"Once you know all the stars by their name," he said, "you can prove you have read all books."

The texts gathered here are meant to stay in the margins of my work. We must leave them their marginal character, even emphasize it, for a freer reading. They owe nothing to the All but, on the contrary, owe all to Nothing. Hence their unquenched desire for All and their primal fear of Nothing.

I would like them to be received as writing of the vertigo where book opens to book.

"Somebody has come and gone. His trace does not *signify* his past, as it does not *signify* his work or his pleasure in the world; it *is* disorder itself being stamped—I am tempted to say *engraved*—with irrecusable gravity."

Emmanuel Lévinas
(*Humanisme de l'autre homme,*
IX: "La Trace")

. . . perhaps this allegiance, beyond the drawn lines, to a disturbing axis,

perhaps the decisive weapon I cannot use?

Words do not fear words, but the text.

. . . this "disorder" which comes to oppose all our natural impulses toward order.

Pages in order, in disorder; here the sign wakes or rests in peace.

"Even a God needs a witness."

Maurice Blanchot
(*Le Dernier Homme)*

Intimate Distance

. . . of this future whose first words I already know.

"To see darkness
the eye withdraws from light
in light"
     Rosmarie Waldrop

     "the other
     the first
     from the plot its purity
        one
     all the clues are mystery to him"
            Anne-Marie Albiach
           [translated by Keith Waldrop]

"An EMPTINESS takes shape and appears
an emptiness takes shape and appears
to explode with its name"
           Joseph Guglielmi

     "He still had the ability left to read a few passages of death, to arrange words in *the other*'s territories."
           Alain Veinstein

"then the noun diminishes
before each utterance
each metaphorical
achievement
some day I shall issue from death
he said
and writing shall go free"

Claude Royet-Journoud
[translated by Keith Waldrop]

. . . of this future whose silence I already fear.

Reb Fu did not find a place in *The Book of Questions*—
how could I have known at that time how much he would
influence my thinking today, at the point where I am now, as
has been the case with so many other rabbis whose existence
I invented and then gradually took my distance from. Reb Fu,
for whom the language of his works—a language salvaged
from language, as it were—had become the only one, charged
full with mystery, had written: "My name is Fu, and it con-
demns me to remain at the threshold of the future, whose first
two letters I have taken on myself."

What could I say, listening to my name after his example,
when all I know of the future is what it obliterates?

I write without imagination, for lack of imagination.
Writing is the opposite of imagining.

The Eternity of Stones

"I have learned that, no matter what I undertake, all I can do is persevere."

Roger Caillois
(Approches de l'imaginaire)

Stone is no doubt the least eloquent, but also, certainly, the most recognizable form of eternity.
On it our buildings rise, our storms break.

When stone becomes transparent or, rather, when transparency turns to stone, all the dreams of the earth can be read.

Eternity plays with eternity in its large, limpid, immobile mirrors.

. . . rampant closure.

What if storms raged also inside the crystal?

PIERRES
by Roger Caillois

"I am speaking of stones older than life, which outlast it on planets grown cold, long after life had its chance to blossom. I am speaking of stones that need not even wait for death, that have nothing to do but let sand, rain, surf, storms and time slide over their surface.

"Man envies their hardness, endurance, intransigeance and luster, their being smooth and impenetrable, whole even when broken. They are fire and water in one transparent immortality, visited now by a rainbow, now by mist. Fitting in his palm, they bring him the purity, the cold and the distance of stars, their several serenities."

I

A book that grows with distance, as a star, with its avowals.

An unusual book.

We must bear this in mind and receive it as if it had crossed vast spaces to reach us. Hence this voice both close and distant, I would even say, all the closer for seeming to come from the darkest of times. Hence this continuity within disruption, as if everything were effaced and reborn in the beginning, a continuity which, in the stone, reveals a blind push toward the invisible, an unparalleled will to endure and complete the cycle.

From the inert to the inert.

Following Roger Caillois, we discover oval and round, double polyhedron and diamond-shape in the stone's polish, its dazzling roads and drunken turns as it were, and feel its mystery and daring.

Medium of multiple representation, of the circle and its metamorphosis *in* the circle, or of the circle and its metamorphosis *after* the circle, the center—knot of truth—always elsewhere.

But everything is true in stone because it exists within death, because it is both the anonymous face of the world and first or last breath of beast and man caught in happy or unhappy succession; because in stone, finally, everything exists before life and after death.

This is why our works want to be accomplished in the image of the humblest pebble, in this common image caressed and worn by sea, rain, and wind, because wear, like wrinkles, is also proof of fatal accomplishment.

". . . the purest profile, the poorest also, but the only one truly necessary.

"In this long acquiescence, this ultimate misery, there is hidden one of the conceivable forms of perfection."

As in a cracked stone, there is beauty at the bottom of a wound.

> "I too, in writing these pages, in assembling my words with freedom and effort, perform, though differently, the same task, a task that was not yet a task or anything of the sort and yet was that of the stones I have tried to describe."

II

(Circle caused by a stone dropped into water.
Ah, shall I one day become master of the uni-
verse by heaving from high on the cliff heavier and
heavier stones into the sea?

At this point of day.
Contested center.)

"The circle we chance on in an agate, if broached by a neighboring circle, gives us the impression of an abortive attempt.

"By contrast, it is all glory if it proclaims itself vast and alone like the sun in the empty sky, on an even field of agate or incandescent crystal. Then it is a marvel."

In the stone, there lies buried the first word of the earth, the infinite of the sign.

The universe was perhaps born of this bold reading.

Nothing in the stone can be lost, from its fixed moment of unfolding, its existence become eternal non-existence.

Did Roger Caillois know from the start that in exploring the universe of minerals as he does he skirts a truth that perhaps always haunted him? Hence a certain appeasement, a kind of serenity—nearly assurance—in his proceedings, which is no doubt felt by all those searchers for the impossible who, rejecting even miracles, denounce, in the name of the idea they serve, imposture wherever it crops us.

His passionate inquiry into the mineral world he has discovered leads him now—perhaps for the first time—to identify with all its fragments, to the point of learning and adopting its writing, to the point of setting up—himself having become the object, the burst stone—an exemplary notebook of correspondences that will push him by and by into defining himself through a new mythology, a metaphysics, a morality, an aesthetic of regions beyond time, where life and death are synonyms.

Thus he confronts writing—his?—inscribed into the void like the burned-out suns that seal the last pages of the book. Book graven in the sign and on its silence; that is, into what—by having been—affirms its absence, into what names itself in order to be.

"In this somewhat hallucinatory vision that animates the inert and goes beyond perception, I have sometimes thought I had before my very eyes one of the ways poetry is born."

III

I see myself again in the deserts of Egypt, looking for pebbles—yellow, sometimes brown—digging them out of the sand, taking them home for the sake of the human face that would suddenly emerge out of their nothingness—an eternal human face that time had modeled for centuries, not mere moments—their face alive against life.

Along amid sand, whose every grain bears witness to an exhausted wind, a desolate world, I was satisfied with appearance, whereas it is inside the stone that the heart of death is merrily at work, where, with a beat of heaven or hell, the closed universe of eternity is written.

Fragment of a Letter

Thank you for your *Cases d'un échiquier*. This "Squares of a Chessboard" has become for me the object, the center, of long reflection.

The preface of the book reveals a movement that is sure of itself, but all the same anxious about every step. It is from this angle that we must now read your books. Inquiry pushes back the boundaries of each one. Beyond, commentary sneaks into the still continuing inquiry, which means new inquiry and new meditation.

There is the object of your curiosity held hardily, implacably—as one grasps a nut, to shell it, a tree, to uproot it—and there is, on the other hand, what glides through your fingers, what can only be grasped elsewhere—or perhaps not at all—and suddenly illuminates us.

There is questioning and, in the end, the despair of rejected answers.

And there is narrative in its own dimension.

The need to probe the given for its secret is characteristic of your thinking: the secret that is not what is hidden, but, on the contrary, what speaks at the deepest level. So that it is the language of the secret that is constantly questioned.

Your approach to things—and beings—goes, almost instinctively, through what hides them.

In order to see, to understand, you start from what does not immediately yield to eye and ear. Patient quest. Indefinite scent within the scent picked up.

It is then that the secret begins to speak, that its words find a privileged place in your books.

Your pace becomes hesitant, as if amazed or frightened at its own horizons.

We are seized by vertigo in the face of the void, where all truth—even that written in stone—dies of having been, of having lasted into death, so that its own, original effacement now seems to us its luminous and coherent manifestation.

Fascinated by what is not, we must appropriate the object by revealing it to itself and others in order to reduce it, as if it were an obstacle to overcome, to surmount. As you had to go beyond the behavior of your brothers, in order to join them in their silence. Masters of annihilation, as of compliance.

Everything connects. Everything corresponds. Man and the beliefs of man, war and celebration, the insect's dance and the immobile stone. The rules of the game are the rules of the universe.

Foray by foray, you lead us to our own confines. We open our eyes on what, for having called on all its resources, remains the mirror of a world we never tire of sounding, while looking at ourselves: world of writing where the world rises and sets, chosen word where we are measured against ourselves and against space as if we had to live—and die—in what rules only in order to be ruled, and we must rule in our turn.

The word is distance within non-distance, that is, the width of a gap that every letter stresses while bridging it. What is said is always said in relation to what will never be expressed. At these extreme limits we recognize ourselves.

. . . but you are hard on the rose stung by the sand. A certain truth, truth taught by the desert, let her get lost in herself, as if she had to be punished for daring to be a flower.

The Moment After

1

"The eye captures what it will destroy. It cannot perceive what escapes death, what is invisible," he said.

"The eye is human. It made Adam mortal.
"When Adam opened his eyes God trembled.
"Adam's fall is the triumph of the eye."
"God is eyeless," he also said.

God knows: He is blind. Man comes to know what his eyes destroy. All knowledge passes through choice. Choice guarantees murder.

"Thou shalt not kill," commands God. Did he hope that man would turn blind again?

"Ah Lord, why make me a murderer by giving me the sense of sight and then damn me for opening my eyes?" wrote a rabbi I met shortly after writing the last page of the *Book of Questions*.

"God created the world on the scale of the creature's glance so that they would die of one another," he had noted.

"God created the world, that is, God created Himself, in order to face up to the eyes of man and to show His power by escaping them," he had noted elsewhere.

The best proof of love the creature could give God was to accept His Invisibility.

The world will go out with the eye. Everything will have been said, as at the beginning.

2

". . . the lethal opening of the eye."

Jacques Derrida

3

The eye is a blank page. It succumbs to seeing.

You turn into writing what you see; what sees you, into reading.

The eye means oblivion. Both oblivion of things seen and the muted glace of oblivion.

You will do nothing. You will disintegrate.

LETTER TO JACQUES DERRIDA
ON THE QUESTION OF THE BOOK

". . . I have regularly tried to put philosophy on stage, on a stage it cannot upstage."

Jacques Derrida

(To speak, to keep silent, already invokes dif-
ference.

Where totality is a blank, the fragment must
also be.

A drop of blood, the book's sun.)

To the incendiary letter we have granted the right
to set fire.
The word is a world in flames.

God burns forever in the four fires of His Name.

O day everlasting within ephemeral day.

"Tonight, like every night, by the light of my candle, I am filling a few unquenched pages with exhumed words.

"God, on the other side of my table, composes His book whose smoke envelops me: for the flame of my candle is His pen.

"What will my book be, shortly, but a bit of ash on one of His pages?

"There is no protected preserve of writing," an unappreciated rabbi, whose name I will not reveal, wrote three centuries ago.

He also wrote: "In every word, a wall of fire separates me from God, and God, together with me, is this word."

The fire cannot die in the word it writes. Eternity of the book, from conflagration to conflagration . . .

There will never be more than one single book promised to the fire to which all books are sacrificed. Thus time is written in the ashes of time, and the book of God, in the mad flames of our books.

(Fire: virginity of desire.)

If, in reply to the invitation to participate in an issue of the magazine *L'Arc* devoted to you, I have decided to address you directly in its pages, it is because I have reached a crucial point in the practice of writing, the heart—and often darkest night—of an incessant questioning of letter and sign (caught at the perilous point of becoming word and book) where I can speak to—or of—others only in the intimate voice of dialogue, a voice charged with all our listening for a voice that, as we know, once broke the silence for itself.

But it is also in order to control my irritation at the fact that, for many, questioning the word has suddenly become a rigged game of surface boldness, a clever appropriation of what cannot be taken head-on.

The code is known, transmitted, and our reading is based on it, on this knowledge, this confidence in the written. A reading called open at the level of the text. But of which text? since, once drafted—of this reading I shall make my writing—the text is nothing but the application of a theory accepted in advance, of a method adopted with all its subtle combinations and schemes, whose consequences for us we cannot even gauge, but on which we nevertheless build our books.

The blank page is not a grid we must adapt to. It will surely become so, but at what price?

Thus the important works of our time are most often approached as part of a current craze and, above all, in terms of what we have gotten out of them and remembered, of what we can cheerfully refer to.

At the farthest outpost of the coast, we erect a lighthouse: stone tower and beacon. We become its honorable keeper, but forget that the only purpose of the beacon is to sweep its beam across the ocean and direct ships through the night toward anchor in safe harbor.

The movement of the book is that of amorous and aggressive waves lit by the pen as by searchlights in the dusk where writing unfolds, and whose sighs, growls, cries, and gasps are recorded from a distance by the lighthouse keeper and the writer.

This is why there is no *pleasure*—alone—*of the text,* nor boredom, terror, or rage. We cannot cling exclusively to one of those equivocal instants when the duration of the text—and otherwise the text would not be text—is sovereign testimony to all the hate and lust felt, all the sperm and blood spurted and spilled by wave and word as our share.

We always start out from a written text and come back to the text to be written, from the sea to the sea, from the page to the page. The ship, too, is perhaps an obsessive word caught by the searchlight, glimpsed, followed, then vanishing, but still haunting us as it haunts the rectangle of paper or the part of the ocean turned white with its passage, with spindrift secreted from a wound.

Light beams! My mind has always connected the image of the lighthouse keeper with that of the fireman up on his ladder: one tries to douse a fire, the other, to light up the sea. Both make us see death.

So many buildings burn beneath the water.
Day and night are one and the same wager of ashes.

Leaving the book, we do not leave it: we inhabit its absence. Likewise, outside their shared space, readable only to them, the keeper at the foot of his lighthouse and the writer away from his desk.

The absence of the book is located both before and beyond the word. But it is also written in the margin of writing, as its erasure.

The gesture of writing is, first, a movement of arm and hand entering into an adventure under the sign of thirst. But the throat is dry, body and thought all attention. Only much later we realize that our forearm on the page marks the boundary between the writing and ourselves. On one side, the words, the work; on the other, the writer. In vain do they search to communicate. The page remains witness to two interminable monologues, and once there is silence on either side, it is the abyss.

Our forearm constrains and inhibits us. All around, words go to waste. We thought that in taking up the pen we could reach a kind of comforting fullness and unity. But afterwards nothing is ever the same. Cut off from ourselves by our own daring, stripped of our belongings, the male gut reaction is to try to master this rebellious voice of ink and to appropriate it.

But the transcribed word, which we naively thought we had arrested and handcuffed, keeps its freedom for the space of its perennial night. Dazzled freedom which frightens and worries us.

Behind the bars, the lines of the book, we watch the word spread its wings in the vast realm that is its own. So that it confronts us first of all with the void; not, certainly, to reduce it, but in order to feel its infinite vertigo. Inside and outside any imaginary enclosure, there begins and ends writing in its perpetual beginning, begins and ends our passionate questioning of an absolute—the book—which is finally but the white ground beyond time on which the shadows of our numbered words have been dancing since daybreak. Death has its heyday where everything remains to be said.

Reading a text involves several degrees of violence; this is sufficient warning that there is danger in the house.

Only in fragments can we read the immeasurable totality. Hence it is with reference to a fabricated totality that we tackle a fragment, which always represents the accepted, traditional part of the totality, yet at the same time renews its challenge of the beginning and, taking its place, becomes the beginning of all possible beginnings that can be brought to light.

The eye is guide and beacon for this fertile "deconstruction" which works in two directions: from totality toward the ultimate fragment, and from the tiniest fragment, through its own rescinding, its own gradual fading into the void of preponderant fragmentation, toward restoration of this very totality. The eye lays down—and is—the law. The invisible claims us behind all that is seen, as if its absence were only what hides at the heart of the manifest—or else hides from us what is nevertheless manifest—and silence, what is unsaid within the uttered word.

To which move, which deportment—or deportation—of writing do we owe our awareness of this invisibility, this silence? What remains to be seen, what promises a voice after silence, fascinates us. The field of writing is twofold. The place of the book is a place forever lost.

Thinking of you, of your questioning and questioned approaches to the book, of your ways that are all one, yet marked by significant twists and turns, as if we could really advance only by accepting, from the start, that we must return to our point of departure, which would be the point of all departures, and asking myself, in turn, the burning question: What is the book? I came across the answer proposed by a kabbalistic rabbi to this most pertinent and pressing question. (A rabbi who, I assure you, knew more about what we now call writing than you imagine, or perhaps knew nothing about it, being more preoccupied with symbolism, but what matter?) An answer that I would divert from its original mystical sense and submit to your literal reflection: that the Book is "what the black of fire carves into the white of fire." Black fire on white fire. Endless consuming of sacred parchment and profane page given over to signs, as if what is consigned— co-signed—to writing were only a play of flames, fire of fire, "word-fires," you said in a recent interview. Confidence in what dies purified to be reborn of the desire for purifying death, thanks to which words add to their own the readability of a time advanced to the "deferred" reading, which we now know is the reading of all reading; time forever preserved within abolished time.

Could it be that for the writer everything happens in a forebook whose end he cannot see, whose end is in his book? But nothing happens that has not already happened. The book is at the threshold. This also confirms your cherished project, your declared course, whose ambition might strike us as paradoxical since it is a matter both of undermining the road and of continuing it, as if it could exist only in and through these successive continuations.

Your "deconstruction" would then simply be starting countless fires, which your philosophers, your thinkers, your favorite writers help spread in their writing: "Valéry reminds us that philosophy is written." Plato, for whom writing is both "remedy" and "poison," a "poison-remedy," considers it suspect, but his suspicion is in writing.

Everything is again set in motion—called into question—by writing. As we *speak*, nothing is ever said so completely that it could not be said over, differently. So that saying is a revelation, with the promise of further saying. Deconstruction functions at this level also, arranging and preparing those moments when utterance splits apart and is neutralized by its reconciled opposites:

"For the unlimited itself has become the limit proclaimed by the neutral affirmation which, speaking always from the other side, speaks in the word."

Thus all your books reflect one another and reflect, back to back, your favorite examples.

You always, and with unequaled rigor, question anything that is taken for granted. What immediately won me over in your writings and the resolve they convey, what commands our respect in your profound attempt to overcome all obstacles and grasp the ungraspable, is the total acceptance of risk that runs through all your work and quickly wears out those who would nail you down. It is precisely the kind of risk that the book in process of being made and unmade forces us to take at each stage of its evolution, its articulation, and its abandonment.

If, starting from Hegel, the "last philosopher of the book and first thinker of writing," from Husserl, Nietzsche, Freud, Heidegger (both closest and most remote), you stop quite naturally on your way as you encounter Mallarmé, Bataille, Artaud, it is not so much, I think, to widen the field of your investigations, of your inscribed and transcribed anxieties, in the mad hope of one day closing the loop, as to increase the sense of the unfathomable in your questioning. For the question of writing truly arises on abyssal ground—the question of being likewise, the two being riveted to one another.

Everything seems to happen as in a game of chess. But what strategy can we resort to when, as with Mallarmé, the chessboard is all white? What game is conceivable where all possibility of play is taken from the players? Here, at this point, begins the adventure.

White is not a color of rest. You know. You have said so. So much virgin blood in whiteness. Desire and wound, kiss and combat fuse in it and drown. Whenever the page we hold on to is not itself the void, it is the "hymen" or "tympanum" of an ecstatic or fearful incarnation of emptiness pierced by the pen. The moment of pleasure or sacrifice consummated, the carnal act continues, and silence is henceforward filled with strange and tenuous sonorities.

A kind of counter-writing carried, however, by writing— its irksome contrary or contrariety, with which it collides and breaks—attempts to lord it where reflexion overflows the foaming wave. But there is already the beach, the sand, the progressive erosion of a reproduced trace that was but the daring imprint of a question left open. The beach is flooded with the "white blood" of the sea; the trace, drowned in blood. Obliteration is but waves of blood on an abandoned wharf all written, all covered with footprints.

"In breaking the silence, language realizes what silence wanted and could not obtain," writes Merleau-Ponty. So it is out of breakage—breakage in death, of death—but of the fatal fissure that renders it mortal while bringing it about, that the question of the book is born. Question put to nothingness, to the void. Question of the void around which swarm mad words that, though impotent, are yet master of the question.

"To question means to be able to wait an entire lifetime," writes Heidegger. To write the question, to question the writing of the question, is even more demanding. It demands going beyond, beyond light, beyond life, into the very light and life, but into their desert regions—are deserts not the dust of questions?—harried to death by panting interrogations, by the recluse clarity of thought and man's arrant word.

Sand responds only to sand, and death, only to death.

Your "margins" are without reassuring contours; your "positions," "disseminating." To hope to be soothed means turning away from you. You burn what stood just outside the flame. Rare, very rare, to live writing with such intensity. "An entire lifetime" is indeed not enough to appease the fire.

You are against all repression and especially, on behalf of the book, against that of the letter; because the letter is perhaps an origin diverted from the origin by its tie to a signified whose weight it must help carry.

So one letter, the seventh, of the word *différence* was secretly, silently exchanged against the first of the alphabet. This was enough to change the text.

You have often explained this new word. It destroys and creates a space where everything is canceled as it faces, as it opens to, its potential difference by deferring it (*différant*); that is, as it opens to what forever opposes and unites it with itself in its textual manifold.

The word "differance" (*différance*) is here a synonym of *mine*. Mine, graphite to draw with; mine, underground riches; mine, explosive.

So the space created by "differance" is at the same time a space for leaving traces, a pyramid to bury the Pharaoh—"pyramid silence of graphic difference," "tomb that we cannot make resonate," but which we have violated, gutted with dynamite, so that going down into the mine means a descent into death, into the night of the word, in order to make off with its riches—and, "playing with a word that has no word, a name that has no name," a black, blinding absence giving birth to signs—"signs represent the present in its absence"—in the time that is a fold in time, a golden time, where writing moves.

Moreover, this word "differance," deferring (*différant*) presence—"when the present does not present itself we signify, we take the detour of the sign. We take in or make a sign"—is here also an equivalent of the Greek coin, *mine*, and—why not—also of *mines* in the French sense of features, play of physiognomy, tics, and all the word denotes.

As "an origin not full, not simple, the structured and deferring origin of differences," "differance" compromises presence by dissociating it from time. The time of presence is not the present tense, but the chance, expectation, and torment of time, the attention paid to time whose vice is writing.

And where it is currency: a place of hoarding and wasting of signs thus simplified.

A single letter may contain the entire book, the universe. Reading the book means, in these pages, excessive reading of a letter that takes us to most remote points. So that it is in the distance where we embrace our differences, in the detours, the backs and forths where we come up against "differance," that the book presents itself as a book printed on an absence disseminated by the page. Absence of an absence dismissed and unraveled by presence.

A glance divides. On one side, fire; on the other, fire. The "black of fire" is the conflagration of evening facing the white conflagration of morning. Between these two fires—for the space of a fraction of a second, the time of fiery nuptials— emerges a familiar face. The sound of words in the book is but the sound made by fire, gestures become the jumbled voices of flames.

> "Philosophical discourse always gets lost at a certain moment. Perhaps it is nothing but an inexorable way of losing and getting lost. Of this also we are reminded by the degrading murmur: *it goes its way.*"
>
> Maurice Blanchot

. . . it just goes its inky way.

Wing and Bond

I

Gravity of certain encounters. So heavy with consequence, but so light to bear
so . . .

(*Distance dizzies the curve; but what center will one day close its circle?*)

. . . this effort of the future to escape time.

Time is memory without object. Forcing time to remember means, as it were, stopping time.

II

Star
of precedence—There is a code of precedence even among
victims. The hangmen have established it with care—
of convention,
of discord,
of decline,
of deputation,
of suffering,
of vigilance,
of rebirth,
star, advent circumvented by death,
—bare.

> (*Star spawn. But it is the most golden, the yellow
> darkened, no doubt with blood, that offends the
> eye; star that once, somewhere in Europe, lepers,
> Jews, and prostitutes were forced to wear; star that
> only the Jews, by ill luck closer to the sky, have
> again lifted up in the middle of this dark century.*)

The price, each time higher, we had to pay to delay just a
little the hour of our annihilation in the book; the cunning but
fierce will to stay the lordly act of creation, to influence from
behind the scene what is about to be written and will not be
written again.

Odds against a spotless life and death.

"If you make a few subtle substitutions among the letters," he said, "*tuer,* to kill, is contained in the words *voir, écouter, parler, écrire,* see, listen, speak, write."

The murder of God is an illegible murder.
On this level, one kills as easily at a distance as at close range.

The mystic's ecstasy is perhaps orgasmic pleasure on a universal scale at the perfect execution of the divine murder.

> *(What emptiness draws me? After the Name and the law, after signs and ashes, ah, of all emptiness, my voice?*
>
> *. . . when the eye becomes audible, and the voice, a resounding glance.)*

In this fear of everything, which makes the clouds turn pale, my desperate voice was but a repeated cry for help. Of this apocalyptic fear of Nothing—terror of ultimate silence— who can free me?

. . . this is why the letter remains the obstacle we must again and again overcome to exorcise our fear. To act in harmony with death means, at this propitious stage, to write under protection.

To die of the voice means to die of what the eye says. To perish by the letter means to perish by what the word sees.
In the first case, the eye is a fire in a well, and in the second, a deep well of fire.

Sand feeds the fire it chokes elsewhere. The desert—at first, a desolate stretch of desire—is formed by myriads of living and dead eyes.

As when flint is rubbed against flint, fire bursts from the friction of the white eye of God against the grey eye of man. For this fire, the universe is a plaything, a game *already played.*

The night of the eye has always tempted our ink. Gold lies inside the word like a constellation of hymns. O song from the far side of death.

"Repudiated by the book, beware of finding yourself empty-handed in the absence of all customary life and death," he had written. "This particular absence is not absence, but the thin oblivion of creation."

> (*"I'll cheat death, I'll have nothing left that could rot."*)

> Bernard Noël
> (*Les premiers mots*)

On Fear, I

"Today I would like to offer this principal explanation of a state I am just getting over: *I am afraid*. I never felt obliged to reveal this truth. My steps are each time more clearly those of a sick man, or at least a man out of breath, exhausted. It is fear that carries me—or horror—of what is at play in the totality of thought.

"God is terrifying unless identified with reason—Pascal, Kierkegaard. But if he is no longer the same thing as reason, I stand before the absence of God. And as this absence fuses with the last aspect of the world—which has no longer anything utilitarian, nor anything to do with future retribution or punishment—the question still remains:

". . . fear . . . yes, fear that only the boundlessness *of thought* can touch . . . *fear, yes, but fear of what . . . ?*

"The reply fills the universe, fills the universe within me:

". . . obviously the fear of NOTHING.

"Clearly, if what frightens me in this world is not bound by reason, I must tremble. I must tremble if the possibility of play no longer attracts me."

Georges Bataille
(Le Coupable)

He was afraid of the black of ink; this was why he wrote.

Most writers, nowadays, are not afraid of anything.

On Fear, II and III

And to be unprotected, that is the risk.

The word is always a false move sidestepped.

> *("Vertiginous space between lines! We need only look at a page of writing," he said, "to realize that our roads are bridges thrown from one point of space to another, from an absence rich in promises, to an absence that is desolate.")*

Born in fear, the Jew dies of fear, however spelled out.

> *("To fear God," he said, "is, in short, to fear the Book.")*

Notes

He had reached *Nothingness* and said to himself that *Nothingness* was perhaps what asks no questions of itself or of others.

He looked right and left and saw nothing, heard nothing.

He no longer asked himself what he was doing there, how and by what detours he had gotten there.

He listened . . .

"Strange, this voice," she said. "Sometimes I recognize it as yours, and then again it seems so anonymous that it obliterates both of us."

> *(The voice was the prey pursued down to its feeblest moan, its stubborn silence.*

> *"Silence is perhaps but six lances held back. The seventh was not accessible," he said.*

> *Silence, s(k)y—lance.*

> *What appears is proven in the crime it confounds, and by that token defined in relation to future crimes. The desire to kill—to kill oneself—is an ancient dream of hegemony inspired by death.*

> *Is our last breath the last word breathed by death—or life—word become ours for eternity? We are born and die in a word.)*

To bring the word home to a point.
What if a circle were but the immense happiness of a point?

"What is an end for you will surely be a beginning in me. Are you not tempted by the happiness of the circle?"

Maurice Blanchot
(Le Dernier Homme)

And if a circle were but the infinite distress of a point?

"And it shall be a vexation only to understand."

Isaiah 28:19

"Like everybody, I wanted to be happy," he said. "Once, happiness was an agate egg in my hand, turned to stone before it could hatch."

(... *fear of the next step*
—so pale the dawn)

Additional Notes

Am I ready to answer the essential question: What is writing?
But it presupposes the power to reply. Who could possess it?

(*Sense?—In the sense of direction, perhaps, from one point-begetting point to another, to how many others?*

We could have gone in the direction of motivated rejection of the sense powered by letters, if death had not already eliminated all freedom of choice, foisting itself on us as the lord of meaning.

The sense and direction of my steps as against non-sense, dead end. God is non-sense and dead end.
All roads of writing lead to Him.

Dead end, that is to say, abyss. Then we realize that, by writing as if the page were empty, we only made words of time sparkle in the black night of dead ends.)

. . . is another dimension not also another destination that the word reserves for both the object of thought and thought itself? Destination unknown until it is reached, at which point yet another destination is assigned, bestowing yet another new dimension?

Of the Recovery and the Reservations of the Text

Is there always useless expenditure of writing, no matter what we write?

The notion of recovery I find, if I turn to my books, in the first trilogy of *The Book of Questions*. And how could one fail to see the notion of reservations, of non-consent of and to the text, in *El, or the Last Book* or, rather, in the "." that is the book's real title, canceling both title and book?

Letters are the chance of the word, as they are also the legible trace of ruined words.

"You drink the Lord's word from a cleverly restored china cup," said a rabbi whom I never gave a name. "But take care that the brew is not served boiling; you would risk shattering your cup and find the native wound of all alphabets."

Breaking a word, letting words play in the breakage of a word, means taking the shortest route to the nearest point. But it also means going from vertigo to vertigo, from void to void in unfathomable accord with the wondrous shortcut. The ultimate phase of writing is perhaps this withdrawal of writing in favor of its operative negation.

(I was rarely worried about "how to say," but, rather, about "how to be silent," Comment-taire, he had noted.)

*

("What you tend to take for wordplay is not simply the play of words. It is an image of their end. Not all words die the same death.

"I have noticed that most words shelter countless other words to which they remain tied through vices and virtues I find interesting to distinguish.

"On the other hand, words live, as we do, in a closed universe, which they cross in all directions on roads they know as the most appropriate. To explore these diverse roads is also thrilling; for they have been laid out by death," he had recently written in a letter.)

The State of the Game
(Michel Leiris)

"More than anybody else I have always found it painful to express myself otherwise than by the pronoun *I*. Not that this should be taken as a sign of particular pride, but for me the word *I* is the structure of the world in a nutshell."

Michel Leiris
(Aurora)

"*To make the naked and screaming world of a bird fallen out of its nest coincide with the magic world of the adventures of language.* This was explicitly my last word at the now remote period when I first noted, on the same sheet, my belief in *the need to make the frivolous play between words coincide with something of vital gravity;* and then expressed my will to *derive from this attitude toward words the means to live more intensely and rules to live by.* A reflection that explicitly affirms a kind of realism, but no less explicitly subordinates morality to poetry since it is in a certain *attitude toward words* that I meant to find both a line of conduct and the source of a richer life. *Morality = rules of the game, that is, that without which there could not be any game. . .*"

Michel Leiris
(Fibrilles)

"A transference takes place from him to us that could make this insistent voice our own, could, with a bit of courage, train this merciless eye on ourselves, while the author's kind backing of life's victims turns into an unconditional rejection of victimization."

Maurice Nadeau
(Michel Leiris et la quadrature du cercle)

"From the bullfight, which offered the example of a tragic art where everything depends on a swerve and the material possibility of a wound, we have come to eroticism, where everything happens at the heart of a similar wound, if it is indeed true that the capital role of a certain lacerating fulfillment is nowhere clearer than in the act of love."

Michel Leiris
(Miroir de la tauromachie)

I

On the scale of the wound.
On the scale of the Game beyond the pale
With *am* for backbone.

A body.
Everywhere, the same body
to whip,
to maim,
to kill.
Everywhere, anarchic states
. . . of song?
. . . of flesh?
. . . of nerves?
. . . of ink?
of one single body.

> *(The body of a typeface*
> *in the book*
> *and the body of a man*
> *in the world.*
> *Abolished borders.)*

Body of child,
of grown-up.
To reach *manhood,*
straddle the body.

> *(A woman for soul;*
> *a dead woman*
> *for a dead soul.*
> *O solitude tracked down.)*

The body of the wound
on the scale beyond the pale

of a body mortally wounded.
And the blood?
What is blood that does not flow?
Perhaps one color too many.
This color is talked of by day.
This color haunts the night.

(A woman-text.
A text-soul.
The universe written in the body.)

. . . this painful absence of the *I* whose presence recomposes face,
    life,
    and age
    which annuls it.

Of such action
the book divests itself.

*

Once the key is found it could open all doors,
except, of course, its own.
Such is the nature of keys.
It is the key.

The nature of keys is to be at the same time word and oblivion.
A forgotten word scrapes the deep. No borders for oblivion.
He remembers everything. He writes down everything he remembers; but forgetting a word—or several—takes a deeper plunge.

All that finally remains of the completed book is a gaping hole,
the same dark hole that is covered by the sleeper's lids.
The silenced word is a killer.

(The hand reaching out of the abyss still tries to write. But what? With what stylus or other suitable point? On what material? On what rectangle of air cut from the void?)

What?—The future word, the hard-pressed future: question asked by the dying past of the legitimized future.

Precision
means effacement.
It is so precise.
It disappears.
Not to hide anything
means to disguise a bit more
—and more than a bit.

Silence is neither at the beginning nor at the end. It is *between.*
Under the yoke,
the word deserts the word.
It labors not to be.

Where no words are, he rummages—madman—for a word.
An endless confession turns to vertigo, black hole,
returns,
as all lights go out,
to the vengeance of horns, the wound.

From the wound to the wound.

II

Arena without halo.
To write with two pens,
two vanquished horns.
Two books—the same?—
One visible, the other invisible.
Book of extremes, book of the middle.

The match begun.
Play of opposing forces.
Play of coverings
torn off.
Cruel nakedness.

Wood exacted by wood.
The voice drifts off.
No help for what runs to fire.

Impossible to give a name to death.

III

The law, a chandelier.
This hall of mirrors is the place of the game,
—games of I am.
Palace of straw.
Smoldering fire.

Every day, books fade;
in dreams, they are made.
Surprise lies in wait at the turn.
And risk.

> *(Furiously the bull of horizons charges to take space on its horns.*
>
> *Day is behind the obstacle, under the starry garment.*
>
> *No total freedom but in nothingness.)*

One wound is enough to feed the open wounds of the sky.
The bull of darkness sees only this one.
To engulf it, night throws itself, prestigious word, on the betrayed star,
on its heart.
Day dies with the first word dared.
—What does it mean then to speak in trick alleys, facing make-believe lakes? What does it really mean to speak in front of muddy backdrops, in this hell of words and chasms?

Silence is the dried blood of the wound.

*

He speaks, and his words follow in his footsteps;
exposes, accuses, explains himself,
develops what can't be developed,
chooses to be his own target
and hits the bull's-eye.
Who is Michel Leiris?
Shoot at your pleasure.
There, there, there, soon the abyss will reopen.

The rules are strict, but in the end very simple.
Toe the line.
Face the inside.
Jump with both feet into the cry.
Keep track of points: vanishing points, points of chance,
of violence, distress.
At this precise hour we are without ties,
but all eyes,
all patience,
all promise.
We tell
and retell
a story of rats.

> *(These small details.*
> *Studious, meticulous memory.*
> *Weight of the book.)*

Proof is never furnished by words,
but by the loyal page,
by the expanse

—the space, you know, the space we dread by day and
night.

Here is his portrait.
And while he writes
he changes shape.

(*Overload of universe.*
So heavy a weight.)

Shoreline. Suicide.
No day without end.

IV

Nights without night

Enthroning of the beheaded.
Statue of fevers and chills.
On condition of never
splitting up solitude.
Make habit concur
with fullness.
Stones of alliance!
The last, who will toss the last?
All around, unappeased absence,
equivalence of forms,
hand modeling desire.

Could it be that a statue is only a frozen shudder from the
far side of enthralment?

Forehead against forehead.
Miserable dogtag underfoot.
Desolate waterfront.

How far, tell me, how far, in the odd hours, goes the
ocean's rage?

Continents
blighted,
turned to dust.

A myriad dead shellfish, our words.

To have the ear of the sand, share the glory of pebbles.
Smooth to a fault, the unhooped night.

Aurora! Aurora!
Inseparable mornings
of pact
and death.

"Aurora! Aurora! face purer than a spark or a probe
sounding the desert, it is your wondrous tongues of flames
that speed the pace of the vagabond sun. It is your silvery
dress and blazing hair, it is your mouth, pink crater giving off
fleeting and crazy words amid the slag of intelligence, it is
your cool and firm hand with nails of strange, shimmering
beasts that attract this head that has nothing left but a tuft of
blond hair!"

Michel Leiris
(Aurora)

V

"There is the steel of pain
there is danger's red"

Michel Leiris
(Haut Mal)

(One time.
It is enough, this time
of capture,
this accessory
outside-time.
Brightness of body.)

Marvel of love
O woman stretched out
to multiply.
To come. To agonize.
Out of some night
or other,
out of silence
or feast.
The body's in charge.
Death loses patience;
for all death is love.
Sign the unfolded page of night
with the propitious night of signs.
Haut Mal, King's Evil, once poetry
had its very own sun:
this sun. . .

VI

(*Biffures:* Erasures
Fourbis: Thingamajig
Fibrilles: Root Hairs

A pale light
in the East,
like a fresh line.
A bowstring.)

VII

(Far slope: the neutral.)

The Unconditional
(Maurice Blanchot)

Neutrality is in some way the nerve of the knot.

The knot resists the blunt pressure of the rope. It is pure resistance, active indifference.

The unconditional is not just another form of the neutral, but, rather, the neutral beyond all form, on the side of *Le Très-Haut,* The Most High, the trap.

Unknot the neutral. Push back the borders of solitude into the boundless.

An unconditional out-take of the book.

"With what melancholy, with what calm certainty he felt that he could never again say: 'I.'"
Maurice Blanchot
(L'attente L'oubli)

Unconditional presence, absence. Everywhere always the same emptiness.

"Non-present, non-absent, it tempts us in the same way as what we can encounter only in situations no longer there, except—except at the borderline: situations called 'extreme,' assuming they exist."

Maurice Blanchot
(*Le pas au-delà*)

"Men search for themselves in their unconditional foreignness."

Emmanuel Lévinas
(*Humanisme de l'autre homme,*
IV: "L'étrangeté de l'être")

Ocean beyond all oceans, absolute.
I am carried by rhythm—by ritual.
All conditioning undone by writing.

No tense to conjugate us.
No temples pale in pallor.

"To answer for what escapes answerability."

Maurice Blanchot
(*Le pas au-delà*)

Bitter ambiguity of the unconditional. To the conflict of conditions, night contributes its offering of a tiny star, and the sea, a handful of salt.

"Writing as a question of writing (a question that carries the writing that carries the question) does not allow you to maintain the same relation to being—understood as tradition, order, certainty, truth, any form of taking root—that you have derived from the world's past, a province you were given to manage in order to strengthen your 'I,' even though it had been fissured from the day the sky opened on its emptiness."

Maurice Blanchot
(Le pas au-delà)

You will accost the unconditional where life is the verb *to live,* and death, the verb *to die;* where all motion, all action, all silence, mobility and immobility, breath and lack of breath, are only the senseless, excessive, infinite approach of a verb in the infinitive; as of any unsubdued word, of the name, the knot, the inedible almond.

O how the bidden threshold slides into the threshold forbidden.

"A bit of light still filters through the words."

Maurice Blanchot
(L'attente L'oubli)

In vain shall we have tried to encompass limitless verb and time in the daring book of our limits, in the half-light of shards.

I

(Wish, wave, sail.

Absolute negative.

Imperious perpetuity.)

We are bound by the book or, rather, by what wants to become a book, but *will never be one.*

"A story? No, not a story, never again." The story consists in permitting to tell, allowing it to come.

No story is taking place. There is no place here for a story.

Your stories leave the grooves of storytelling and become sheer discovery of speech at its end, in its last inscribed, audible moments.

Linear, fragile, insidious writing. And disarmingly limpid. Nowhere the least excess. What a lesson! And what an enthralling mirror! Reassuring in some ways, but only seemingly. Like transparency.

How to tell our bonds? By refering to exile, perhaps, which is the center, the oil spot.

Writing is always repressed.

On the other side of life, of night: the book.

(Will this questioning of death through the mediation of the book, through the minute saved and proposed as such by writing, ever find rest? Writing keeps up the illusion that rescue is near. But fire cannot save us from fire; or cold, from cold; on the contrary, they perpetuate.)

We are also bound by silence, the insolence of the dry well, the long asides of sand to sand.

We are bound by the white of the sign's whiteness and the black of the sign, become legible at its whitest.

We are bound by the torment of thought at the edge of the unthought; by the impossibility of saying and being said.

We are bound by centuries of anxiety and the small glimmer of light, on which our masculine energies converge: *dissidence*.

> *("Is the well not the inkwell?*
>
> *"Friend, do not dip your pen for more than a moment. You might drown with it: for your body is in your pen.*
>
> *"But how much more horrible the death threatened by the well run dry!" wrote a sage encountered in* The Book of Questions.)

We are bound by the sayings of the sages in my work and by what, once out of the book, they left unformulated.

> *(. . . is dissidence not also the distance that saying takes from what is said everywhere, the space that necessarily breaks with both letter and voice, whose discourse always strikes us by its mute eloquence captured only in the silence of margins and promised beaches? Distance of sand from sea, of sky from earth, inherent in their very nature; distance to which we owe that we breathe, move, express ourselves beyond expectation, beyond oblivion?*

"I do not hear their words or see their lips move. And yet I know they are talking. All they have to tell each other is articulated by their eyes in love," said Sarah.

Lovers' words are molded out of undefinable silence.
We are bound by the greater silence of lovers, of martyrs, of the dead.)

Roadstead and *Story:* two obstacles outline their contours. Two coarse markers. Beginning and end. So we can safely dock our small craft. But if the obstacle is of silk, of air, of smoke, which boatman, which reader taking refuge here, would feel safe with his goods?

There is no end to the voyage, nor any prelude. No resemblance whatever between writer and mariner.

The home port—unacceptable.

All books answer the questioning of a single one.

The story develops on several levels, with different degrees of connivance. Hence the gap between what is—never altogether—said and what is—never altogether—perceived. So that it is in what is expected, forgotten, regained, and lost again that the text takes its written form.

Who can tell the immediate future of this kind of writing or draw up a record of its readings?

(I watched graceful, transparent fish move through the water, some below the others, between the rocks. Suddenly they all gathered at the same level. This, I thought, is also the way of the sentence in those fraternal moments of writing when word lines up next to word for the same chance destiny while death besieges the sea.)

II

A work beyond recovery. Could it be unfamiliar with the ardently expected return, which for us was a "Return to the Book"?

Return to the *reading* of lips. Then everything would be no sooner pronounced than read.

There is always a book ready for the advent of the book.— The book follows.

A work beyond regeneration, ripened in spray mist.

But time is not at stake here.

O death of thousands more, of a thousand morrows.

There would still be sun if everything renounced the light.

A work beyond reduction to cloud, mirage, message, usage, suffrage, ravage. . .

How tell our bonds?
Death sheds our ballast.
Distance fogs
the universe.
Nothing pits us against Nothing.

In this pond,
remoteness of times
and present
stagnant.

The obstacle rules, not the waters, only our passage.

(Can we be healed by repetition? Repetition cancels the book.

Without book, cut off from all words, ah, will we finally die at the unexplored edge of the desert unhaunted by a single sign or sound, at the exploded confines of desire?

III

A line
so fine.
On the far side,
on the near side,
the abyss.

Undercut the rock: blunt tunnels cut in parallel.
Themselves.
Itself.

Elodea, from *helodes,* aquatic plant on a new continent,
spreading so fast.
Death has chained the pond.
To render unto water the water.

(Give the letter h *back to the word,*
the hatchet to the liberator.
Opt for the better spelling.)

Initial cells. Between the two extremities of the stem, radical experience of Nothingness.

The white there.
The page
after all this white.

("*. . . but the real experience could be reduced to the absurd proposition:* I must be there because I must not be there.")

Pierre Klossowski
(Le bain de Diane)

From the wound claimed by the mine to the anonymous writing at the bottom of the water.

*

"Theory of the conditional: (Theology) Knowledge that only God has, of what could have been under certain conditions, in certain circumstances."

Littré

No theory of the unconditional,

only
A TEST

of sight
—between see and say—

of oblivion
—between say and do—

of silence
—between night and blood.

*

First, great freedom: insubordination to the real in favor of
an *unconditioned* reality.
Freedom of a perverse absolute.

A riddle, a point.
Always at the end of a book.

An unconditional fire,
a fault,
a fact—we exist?

Posthumous life to which he opposes—out of nowhere—
his own posthumous life:

> *(Life in suspense*
> *serpentine*
> *in the void.)*

All presence is conditioned; unconditional, only infinite
absence.

Does the sound of the sea prove the existence of sound or
of the sea?
And the silence of the sky?

Dependent on *saying,*
on the cry.

> *(Elodea, lavish speech. Difficult navigation from*
> *what is to what is.*
> *No flora in these parts, fruit unknown, blank*
> *boundlessness, famine.)*

Discordant sea. Accord sealed on the far side of day.

The infinite can be defined in infinite terms only.

Death lives on the void. Dying means, in some way, living the void.

To exit from our vocabulary in order to let it write us on nothingness.
Then writing would mean keeping the exits clear in the condemned word.

Step out of the ranks
finally? RAMBLING.

The trace picked up proved our grace.

*

    THE UNCONDITIONAL IS SAYABLE IN WHAT CANNOT BE SAID, THINKABLE IN WHAT CANNOT BE THOUGHT.

Unconditionally vibrant.
A STRANGER.

> *(What could have conditioned him? Presence? But if presence is itself absence? The book? But if, in the end, the book only words its own hopes? Time, breath, gait, questioning? But if these are to our discomfort denied by eternity, universe, wandering, affirmation?*
> *We would have to tackle the sun, the solar law, the eye, the immensity of day and night, our anarchically diffuse and paltry knowledge. . .)*

Such knowledge is not for us.
For us: not-knowing.
Knowledge severed from knowing
in which knowledge wallows.

Proud indifference of frigid thought.
Inertia at the highest level of knowledge.

Mixed into the sand like a grain, to exist only through it.
Here, being blind means seeing all.

Purveyors of drugs
—for voyeurs—
be off.

Here, being blind means being sober.

Knowledge is extreme poverty of power.
O passive flatness, O dead sea.

Another day, a like day, wounded by a moment's writing.
What if tomorrow were to reject, violently, its metamorphosis?

Compatibility.
Incompatibility
of acts, functions.
Sometimes a word, an eagle.
Night holds on to its holiday trimmings.
Day: site of Nothing.
Face against face,
Page after page.

*

They turned their spotlights on the eroticism of the word,
but it was the eroticism of silence that dazzled.

> ("*The most erotic minute is the chalky minute of
> silence,*" *Yukel had noted.*
>
> "*But lust is waves of sweat foaming with sperm,*"
> *said Yaël once.* "*Unforgettable nights. You write
> with sperm on the beautiful moist pages of my glis-
> tening body.*" *And right after, as if in a dream:*
> "*Lust is the mortar binding the stone.*")

Fear of love is fear of the day.

"All of love is in the silence after life. My love begins with
that silence," Sarah had written.

The hand knows it will one day brandish the parchment of
the last judgment.
Cut off all hands if you refuse to be judged.

This law was the law of the book; but how much abuse in
its application.
Spittle!

IV

"*In mortmain:* Man on condition. Ancient term of juris-prudence. Applied to Jews, who could bequeathe their possessions only to direct descendants, and whose legacy, in case they died without children, fell to the Lords.
In France, Jews were serfs in mortmain.
In Franche-Comté, a free man who has lived for one year and one day in a house in mortmain becomes a slave."

Littré

The book, a house in mortmain? What has become of the thick walls of our dwellings?
No roof, no walls
left.

Serf, Jew of the book. How could the man who entered my house know it belonged to me, since I live in a word that belongs to no one? And yet he was made a slave through my fault.

Not even my children could benefit from what I have to leave. I give my all and this *all* is but ashes of countless nothings.

We hew stones as we hew our death.

What resists is what happens to die a more dignified, more ample death.

All this time, death had us under its yoke, provoking the future with its arrogance.

The book, have we chosen to live in it?

You said: "Both writer and reader are in the book, and *both are dying.*"

Serfdom, at the discretion of the book.

L'arrêt de mort, the death sentence, is pronounced by the first word, implacable judge.

The mirror misleads knowledge.

*

There would be the event. However, does the event exist?
There is the white space *before* the event and the white space *after.* But who could tell them apart?
So the event is perhaps only the unexpected shattering of the white space within the indefinite space of the book.

Fascination of the worst: the invisible.

> *(Where are you when you talk too much? In which privileged spot of the globe and the mind?*
> *. . . and when you do not talk? . . . and when you are talked to?)*

This noise heard by no one. I hear it. This red liquid that flows under the skin, seen by no one. I see it. I drink it.
Ears, eyes. O unquenchable thirst.

Soon I will die of having drunk all my blood. I shall perish of having seen and heard myself.

For all my blood is ink. For ink is my blood.

Where does my body begin? In which dark, hidden place was born the written, legible adventure of my body?

As I was lying there, I thought for a moment I would never stop growing.

The time has come for us to lose even the support of the last day.

"There cannot be any book," said Yukel. "For if the book existed it would have stopped haunting us. What exists is our obsession with the book. Every book written is an effort to come free of our obsession with the book."

Is God merely a separate sign, pure vocable?

Ah, to reduce the text to one word. To render the page to this unique, transparent vocable.

*

Bound(less). Less lessens all bounds.

"In writing you 'lessen' Nothing. Then fear has no more limits," Yukel had put down in his notebook.

Could God be my fear? As much as he could be the infinite of Evil?

Fear. A whole vocabulary trembles inside this timorous word.

Unable to stand the *unthought* we take shelter in thought, as if it were a stranger to the former.

The danger, here again, is emptiness, the unthought.
Latent risk.—Will I write the unconscious, exciting expectation of risk?

The word works in blackest darkness.

. . . infinite attention paid to infinite expectation.

> *(Farther, farther still. Distance is the cradle of expectation.)*

Fasciated infinite of a shell of air.
Air means conquest of the infinite.
Everywhere the selfish sea, sea without salt, without water, sea of rotten algae, cadavers of thought.

Would that my thinking were always airy.

Celestial compost, each star a grain of it, O wisdom of serene constellations.

V

"Knowing is enough to mislead us. As if knowledge were given to us only so we could know what we cannot bear to know."

                                              Maurice Blanchot

"To stop on the road would mean to favor this road at the expense of another. I move on, unsure. The future, I now know, leaves no trace."

"And yet you will die on the road."

"What is death where there are no more roads?"

"Perhaps expectation, perhaps also oblivion of roads; night of unsayable and absurd wandering."

(Erasing His Name, God multiplied the roads.
So the chosen people became a people of nomads.
Millions of unknown names have buried the
Name.)

VI

"So white was the cry we had reason to think that pain simply meant feeling stages of whiteness."

"The crematorium ovens were not their only crime, but surely the most abject, in full daylight, in the abyssal absence of the Name."

"Not the hour, not the century, but immortality sacrificed."

"You will love, as they were hated, at white heat, in dispute."

> *(Even the humblest question shows excessive pride.*
> *We shall turn away from the question.*
> *Without gesture, without voice, we shall obediently enter the inextricable maze of death's radiant whiteness.)*

VII

Let everything be white in order to be birth.

(White, the murmur.
White, the petal.
White, departure.
White, erasure.)

So many shades within white! Liquid white, white powder.
How many nuances within white! From the glacial white
of mountain peaks to the warm white of the paper reserved
for His Name.

V'herb

Day after day, my writing has consisted in savagely weeding out intruding grass and roots; then in refusing to fertilize my land by slash and burn.

No survival in this death, but an implacable sur-death.

To challenge gardens means to challenge what flatters nose and eye.

No perfume in the desert, no delight; only the acrid smell of plundered eternity, the deconsecration of glorious forms; *action brought against the eye.*

Any moment of life has its scent. Once out of the body, life smells of nothing.

"A pestilential stink of rotting meat, this is the border between life and death," he said. "There is no other demarcation line. Luckily, nothingness eliminates all smell. But who would have supposed for a moment that, secretly, the void was the herb's fatal hope?"

Does continual writing signify hope even where hope is written off?

You no longer expect anything, but you still write.

I write, bending down to the very roots, scorched by the cry of soil forsaken by water.

I write in the dust of roots once green, of words once black, of stones and
years now grey.

"Grey, all vocabulary," he said. "Grey, the books of time."

Write to shake off the dust; write at the peak.

> *(Never have you paid particular attention to dust, yet it is the limit of time abolished.*
>
> *You write one last time in the dust because you cannot free yourself of words. You still move within your limits.*
>
> *You work in the vineyards of death, but you refuse to die this early.)*

Once, it was all yours, the circle.
Once, it was all yours, the point.
But when?

Dust! Air spreads its own suffoction.

Every grain in the lot has chosen its victim.

Inside and *outside?* Perhaps two colors of ashes.

"Dust," he said, "is our origin.
"I shall have written with dust alone; for there are no words, only the dust of lost characters from which we have composed an alphabet."

(Its smell—of yesterday, of tomorrow?—is familiar.

I feel it with congesting lungs
  as I watch for the moment when I inevitably go down
    into the murky deep of the air.)

What else can I teach you of the beginning,
except to expect
neither help nor miracle.

All this dust we cannot shake off, but which, rather, thickens with time, with time. . .

Modeled from dust, the world fears the wind.

> *(Century after century they followed their courses until, our eyes lifted up to death, we saw their bodies—O splendor of their last couplings—turn to diamond dust forever.*
>
> *"And oblivion will turn you to stone and dust of stone for all eternity," he also said.)*

The Absoluteness of Death

I

Death means alliance.

". . . but here we reach the point where true being
is altogether confined and *defined* by its *end,* where
consciousness, master of itself, joyously destroys
all possibility of escape and hypocrisy. Reduced
to itself, stripped of all the haphazard tinsel that
disguised it, the inner will rallies, radiant, to the im-
minence of death. It takes death as its accomplice,
as if it could unveil itself to our eyes only on a
ground of nothingness, in the brief moment when
the hero gives way to the dark before fusing with it.
Because there is no more exit toward a future—
which means there is no way of 'thinking elsewhere'—being settles on the perfect fullness of *here*
and *now.* It mounts and makes firm its power,
which henceforth nothing can wrest from it."
Jean Starobinski
("Montaigne et la dénonciation du mensonge,"
Dialectica, vol. 22, 1968)

The Lovers

"At this point, devotion turns into sacrifice on an asymptotic curve toward the absoluteness of death. To live only for the beloved soon becomes living only through the beloved, having ceased to live for and through oneself. A profound liberation which, in turn, gives our very life a marvelous ease, joy and fearlessness.

. . . The passionate lover . . . thus becomes a living dead, kept alive by a kind of artificial respiration she craves—a potentially dead woman whose every moment of life now depends on her beloved. To express this state is to repeat constantly (in a most undiplomatic manner) that she would die if her beloved turned from her. It is to proclaim that life is a conditional gift received from him. . . His defection, say, rather, its mere distraction, would doom the woman en-

I read, in parallel:

"At this point, devotion turns into sacrifice on an asymptotic curve toward the absoluteness of death. To live only for (the book) soon becomes living only through (the book), having ceased to live for and through oneself. A profound liberation which, in turn, gives our very life a marvelous ease, joy and fearlessness.

. . . (The writer) thus becomes a living dead, kept alive by a kind of artificial respiration he craves—a potentially dead man whose every moment of life now depends on his (book). To express this state is to repeat constantly (and in a most undiplomatic manner) that he would die if (the book) should turn from him. It is to proclaim that life is a conditional gift received from it. . . Its defection, say, rather, its mere distraction, would

trusted to him. So, in extreme devotion, sacrifice and suicide become possible, but, we suspect, it is also the ultimate weapon of possessive desire, of grasping greed. Mme de Staël and her heroines contrive to barter the *nothingness* they face into the small change that allows them to preserve the whole of being."

Jean Starobinski
("Suicide et mélancolie
chez Mme de Staël,"
Coppet Colloquium

doom the man entrusted to it. So, in extreme devotion, sacrifice and suicide become possible, but, we suspect, it is also the ultimate weapon of possessive desire, of grasping greed. (The writer) contrives to barter the *nothingness* he faces into the small change that allows him to preserve the whole of the book."

II

I am going to die, Yukel, I must, in this book we do not have time to finish writing.

I am dying within myself for this unfinished book.

How many untouched pages before us!

Yet are they without wrinkles, as empty as we think?

It is as if a shadow of an unhappy hand so heavy, so cold, it seems lifeless at the edge of the table.

How heavy this hand at one extreme of my body! How heavy this heart in the moist hollow of my hand!

The book could have been ours. I thought it would be. I hoped so. This was clearly madness. What life could appropriate the book all for itself? Death could, perhaps. Then all these still untried pages would yield to the accrued number of words that nobody could read within time.

A book for no one, at the end of a love without frontiers.

Tomorrow is another moment of the book to be deciphered.

This book stripped of words, Sarah, nevertheless contains our story because it is a book written by death, and we have been dead from the moment we lost our name.

A thick blanket of snow covers our words. They are so distant, so forgotten by our brothers that they are perhaps no longer even human words, but distorted echoes of our buried screams.

The absence of the book consecrates our absence. Like me, you are alive only where we no longer are, that is, where all mirrors lie shattered at the foot of a single one, behind which we stand, immobile.

The void we are examining is not that of the book we are quietly plunging into. It is the void of their book, Sarah, of which we are a transparent page, hostile against any resurgence of symbols, any belated flowering.

Out of the silence of centuries, discrete words will, one day, surface for us and then for those who have gradually learned to read us in the void. Our book is for tomorrow.

> *(Does the book, here, stand for love? The book is an object of love. The manifestations of love in the book are the hugs, kisses, bites of sentences, words, letters, and, outside the book, an unveiled passion for the written wound, fertile lesion whose lips we spread like a vulva to allow in the sperm of death.*

"Your parts, woman, are the white abyss of the book which once bled for an unheard-of word that the flood of our words has since carried off," he said.

But hate and envy are also in the book: hate and envy of God quickened by an undeciphered text, a text under the text, for which the latter exhausts and consumes itself.

There is fire in the page to kindle and snuff its whiteness, eternal morning of the first, the only, book.)

From the terrace of my hotel I watch how countless birds—the waves—die with wings spread over the water.

And I say to myself, this must be the way books die, given that they begin with words taking wing toward the sky.

At times, one will make a powerful effort to rise into the air, but immediately fall back, making a hole in the sea.

Our graves are not those of words, nor those of fish or seabirds, graves of moving eternity. They disdain and disturb the order of time.

"There is no end to the sea or the book," you said. "Words unwind the transparent thread of days in the continual back-and-forth of their life and death left to themselves.

"Though the pen grow weaker and weaker, the book nevertheless writes, in white letters, on to its end."

Making a book could mean exchanging the *void of writing* for *writing the void*.

(Nothing is alike anymore. Remains what is to be remembered, that is, what is still standing between what was and what is no more: simulacrum of object, of language, of light.

Writing is the dawning solitude of the letter.)

"Yes, I am this murmur, as you also are this murmur, yet always separate from one another, on either side of the murmur that says nothing, but, ah, degrading"—"marvelous"—"noise saying nothing but: *it goes its way.*"

Maurice Blanchot
(Le pas au-delà)

2

Doubly Dependent on the Said

. . . as if all the truth transported by the book—this portion of dark where the light wears thin—were but an approach to death, for which writing is both a piece of luck and a misfortune; a death become ours through every word, every letter, through sounds and silence, where sense is only what makes sense of the adventure. As if, moreover, in order to make sense, this adventure needed the deep sense of words, their multiple meanings, which are but focal points of their radiance.

Thus the book, borne by its words, lives their intimate life and dies of sharing their death.

Thus we are first led on and then forsaken by every fraction of a second of our life. So that we can finally bear witness only to this forsaking.

Fore-Speech

"Fire establishes a classification."

Francis Ponge

"Something perfects something inside me."

"The comparable gives way to the incomparable."

Henri Michaux

The Bet

To bet on the bet, not on the choices that condition it.
To opt for certain risk rather than hypothetical gain.

To save the bet from choice: *reality of writing.*

A wager for the sake of the wager—like desire for the sake of desire, love for the sake of love, adventure for the sake of adventure.
The object no longer the stake, only the pretext.

Where nothing can lead to results, any result is proof both of the foreseen lack of result and of Nothing.

In the beginning was Nothing, which has no beginning.

Intimate Distance, II

"Ein Wort, mit all seinem Grün,
geht in sich, verpflanzt sich,
folg ihm."

Paul Celan
(Schneepart)

Could it be that distance has its stages; proximity, its milestones?

There are two kinds of discoveries in literary matters: the work that is complete in its very incompletion—an incompletion ineluctably carried to term—and the work that has come only halfway toward its always deferred completion. Both interest me; one for the road covered, the other, for the road that remains.

So many quotations of authors I see, so many notes taken day after day, asleep in my drawers.

There are the few writers, thinkers, dreamers, poets who opened my eyes, and there are those who have allowed me to keep them open. There are those I avidly keep reading and rereading and those whom I read only in snatches. There are young authors I have come close to these last years and older ones from whom I have gradually taken my distance.

A shared word is always new.

"Our blood to silver this mirror:
writing."

Jacques Dupin
(Dehors)

"Lines and lines of white, eyes drawn into the
distance."

Emmanuel Hocquard
(Album d'images de la villa Harris)

"Behind this mask is the voice we
would have to imitate. . . And the face
of another we would have to tame."

Gérard Macé
(Leçon de chinois)

"The time has come to do my self-portrait."
Jacques Roubaud

"There is no writing
but blurs time."

Jean Laude
(Le dict de Cassandre)

The book's glance: glance of closed eyes.

"Keep to your book."

Franz Kafka
(Journal)

The Point

"I am nearing the end. With each breath, the thin air of my finiteness swells my lungs. My relation to the infinite goes through each of these stages, these deadlines. I live by my innate ability not to stop dying," he said.

The Hebrews compared the present to a point, seeing it as the end of the past and the beginning of the future.

In *The Book of Questions*, I defined the point as the smallest circle—a new center. Point of prelude and end, but which end? No doubt the one every beginning leaves behind: a heap of charred stones from a building on fire.

Writing knows nothing of the present. The first word breaks with the past in order to face, virgin, the demanding future.

Steeped in fresh ink.

All becoming rests on an unknown quantity which is no sooner known than it turns back into the initial mystery.

The future might just be ignorance of a past to discover. This ignorance is true knowledge tracing its royal road through the night, among the stars.

This night remains to be reached.

The contradictions that feed our questions do not lead to nothingness but to the unsayable that we must put into words.

"A word often has a meaning which leads to another,

which leads to a third, which makes us realize we are still at the threshold of the word.

"To exhaust all meanings of the word in a single one, this is the writer's task," he said.

Within the All, there is disintegration of the All, as within being there is fatal crumbling of being. What future for this? Yes, what is, finally, perpetuated?

> *("The practice of impermanence is tied to the practice of the question: it is realized by getting out of the self, by abandoning all the referential and denotative finality that belongs to the imaginary, by the humility of its very necessity within its limits, by inventing a death that is, after all, the tragic game of life."*
>
> Adolfo Fernandez Zoïla)

Wrinkles of the Day

". . . this unknown quantity at my disposal, for balance."

René Char

To raise the question to the level of the sun, the source of clarity.

What you expect from others you must ask of yourself.
The sun is the celestial present of night to night.

"The next heart takes its position."

René Char

Which

"We may completely take apart the human being. We may identify the elements of thought and will. But we shall always encounter—and not be able to resolve—this X I have come up against. This X is the Word, which burns and devours those who are not prepared to receive it."

Balzac

(Louis Lambert)

"You know," he said to me, "that Mallarmé had assembled a great many little slips of paper whose purport intrigued his contemporaries to the highest degree. He countered questions about them with absolute silence and gave orders that they be burned after his death. All I can say is that during the time in my life when I worked with him on the translation of Whistler's *Ten o'Clock*, I one day entered Mallarmé's study to find him at his desk with one of these tiny papers in his hand. He was silent for a few moments, then murmured as if to himself: 'I dare not write even this any more, I still surrender too much.' Standing close by, I read on the slip the single word: 'Which.' He put it back among his papers, and I never had occasion to learn more."

Francis Viélé-Griffin

to A. Rolland de Renéville

(The word is not the beginning, but the limit. It is an antecedent end, accession to the fatal risk man will accept to run.

Beginning and end of the written are but both-
ersome obsessions of the word, its false mobility.)

Perhaps all I have attempted in my books is to get rid of the burdensome "I" in favor of the almost anonymous "We."
To write means perhaps nothing but gradually reaching this anonymity.

To be the other and permit him to be me: dark road of anonymity.

"There will always be a crumpled page to resist the hangman, with a humid word like a belated tear dropped on it.
"I am the transparency of this word," he had written.

"Plant a tree in the fertile soil of your blood. The soul, too, needs shade," he said.

"Good attracts good as evil attracts evil: infinite pull," he also said.

"The book," he had noted, "does not open from left to right or from right to left, but from top to bottom: one page in the sky, one page in the dust."

The good, in the eyes of the better, is the disappointment of the good.

"My bed was flat stones on the road.
"Do you find this just?"

"It is just because you have never lacked for a stone to enjoy your night's rest.

"There are no miracles except for the poor."

"What shelter can we suggest for people who do not know peace?" he used to ask.

He was told: "As long as night remembers night, and day, day, they will not find respite."

Carte Blanche

To leave it to the writer to comment on his work means, in a way, to take him out of his books.

On the surface, this might seem paradoxical, because we ask him to do it precisely to help us enter his books, as a host would help his guests.

However, facing the text, the writer is in the same position as the eventual reader, the text always opening up to the degree that we *are able* to read it. It is each time the *text of our reading,* that is to say, a new text.

The writer writes himself in reading, the reader reads himself in what is written.

You will surrender your name to passage.

Wide, the margin between carte blanche and white page. Nevertheless it is not in this margin that you can find me, but in the yet whiter one that separates the word-strewn sheet from the transparent, the written page from the one to be written: In the infinite space where the eye turns back to the eye, and the hand to the pen, where all we write is erased even as we write it. For the book imperceptibly takes shape within the book we will never finish.

There is my desert.

> *(The difference between the author's reading and that of the reader is perhaps that the author alone is responsible for taking the risk of a first, blind reading through which the book takes shape,*

whereas the text appropriated by the reader gives the book a chance for other readings and unsuspected dimensions.

So: a reading before the book, by the author, and a reading after the book, by the reader.

On the bottom of the sea, an undeciphered text fascinates the writer. So daring his dives! And if the words brought to the surface are black it must be because, as with the frightened octopus bloated with venom, once caught, ink is their dazzling weapon.

Reading is a daughter of light.)

With every step thought to bring it closer to its model, the book destroys more of it.

O solitude of signs.

The Merits of Comfort:
Its Portion of Night

"If God is a fiction—a supreme fiction—who will authenticate the word?"

Georges Auclair
(*Convergences?*)

What should I privilege in my books unless what escapes privilege?
"Morning of discomfort; black hell of comfort.
"At night, I rest on myriad needles of fire.
"Stars. Stars. . ." he wrote.

Thought grows in the discomfort of its shadow.
Ah, to float like that! Buoyed up by the dark.

There are trees unknown to the seasons, whose fruit are meant for us. Trees of petrified forests with large leaves like strange tombstones. Lie down under them.
Here, we die in stages.

As tears by the infinite, or drops of water, by time, "You" is cut off from "I," but joined to it for one and the same fate.

What is meant to flow inherits fluidity. This is its merit.

We can conceive only of unity. Disintegration is internal.

The book is opened by the moment. It is surprised by eternity with its trumps of dark and light.

You write on two distinct levels, in two irreconcilable times.

Punctual—death is always on time, the motionless time of the past or the still time of the future.

Marble, our broken mast.

The universe is a fixed point. This point is God.

Everything moves for having never moved. Write, write. *Only writing is motion.*

As long as even one single person approves, intolerance will go on living its most festive years.

"What is your belated indignation or occasional crying to us?

"Dry your tears. Rush back to your daily tasks.

"You cannot escape your responsibility toward us except by taking refuge in pretexts that acquit you. Washed clean of suspicion. With floods of water."

"Filthy, filthy water," cried the victims.

No matter what you say or do, man, you are implicated. The future will plead for or against you.

We feign to be roused by injustice; in fact, we are roused only by what suddenly, for a moment, disturbs the comforts we enjoy.

"To teach the victims to die with respect for their masters is the hangman's chief worry," he had noted.

Indignation, too, has its accepted—acceptable—degrees. Have we not stressed this enough?

We really pay attention only to ourselves, to our nearest reflection.
The other: an intruder who skews the givens.
He pretends to love the other; loving, thereby, only himself.

Those who rise up against intolerance are often the most intolerant.

"What responsibility do I have toward my neighbor? The kind a tree might have toward the forest.
"*We are planted*," he said.

My neighbor is my face; and I am destroying it.

Taking sides is already a form of intolerance. But how could we escape it?

He claimed to accept me as I am, but refused my returning the courtesy: *he was afraid of being taken for another.*

We try to tie down with words what, with buoyant power, always comes back up to the surface.

It happens, however, that the blue sheet of water is stained with blood.

Pardon is intolerable to the pardoned when the act is justified only by excessive tolerance.

We do not measure goodness by its weaknesses.

To take on another is as difficult as to take on yourself. In this difficulty there is the entire weight of our solitude.

Fraternity does not mean a hand offered to your neighbor. It means a hand that has already gone halfway to meet the friend's hand: a story of happy or unhappy love.

Stay. Even if you are not sure I am here. You will find me.

God's triumph: All absence means presence to nothingness, means awakening to the void.

Thought—like freedom, love, hate—rejects all ties in order to weave its own.

To be tied to what we tie with our own hands, not to what strives to tie us: solidity of ties.

"Do not search behind the morning fog for the hidden sun. The fog is thick enough that you risk gauging your impotence on its daily cruelty," he used to say.

And added: "Grey is crueler than black because it permits hope."

What of ourselves can we hand on? No doubt nothing. But this Nothing is all we own.

Hope is a whirl of dead leaves, a reflection of their gold rustling in the wind.

The Oval

"To bear solitude and not swerve from it."
Didier Cahen

The oval may, after all, be but a circle that has—from negligence, daydreams, forgetfulness?—delayed its closure.

Listening to . . .

Rosmarie Waldrop

Fractured writing, suspended in a space she suddenly refuses to close in on, cut off as if suddenly no longer valid, in order to attempt the cruel task of articulating itself in the unsayable.

Writing charged with emotion brought to intentionally sudden endings, then to take on the imperceptible movement of silence where the echo of vocables fades.

Writing of torment rather than rupture, singularly daring, tenacious, immodest in its most secret moments, but of an altogether classical rigor and uncommon simplicity of tone.

So many virgin paths run through these texts, inviting us.

It is always *elsewhere*—clearly, nowhere, but she does not know this or pretends not to—that beings and things have their chance to be grasped through "words already there," through ever new—similar—names, names that resist obliteration.

And her astonishment that some might follow her where she—now—no longer is for having stayed so long, for having "stayed to see."

Before us, the abyss of unveiling and, behind us, "what is said," that other abyss.

Claude Royet-Journoud

Bathed in silence, tormented by silence that is no longer altogether silence, but last, silent words (last because perceived after all others). Words, then, from the far side of silence, which prolong it only to take its place, words born of the possibility and impossibility of others, of the missed possibility and felt impossibility of others. Last, silent words then, but at no moment are the words silenced. Silent words that mark the silence only to break it, but which, O despair, can never break or even touch it. A white wall that has stopped being wall to be only whiteness of white, transparent, empty; words of emptiness, rather, already more easily grasped through what cannot hold them, what has done nothing but try to hold them. Words, I will add, of all words that are wasted, bruised, abandoned at the edge of silence.

"A strength passes from hand to hand."

It is at this "strength" we need to pause, as we pause, not so much at real obstacles, but at the stretch between us and the infinite—and beyond, a space so vast to the eye, so crushing to thought that we are frightened, a space which, however, is not altogether desert, but a space before or after the desert, for the desert lies at the bottom of each word.

"This is not a book for you." [1]

1. Quotations are from *The Notion of Obstacle,* translated by Keith Waldrop, Windsor, Vt.: Awede Press, 1985.

Joseph Guglielmi

To use all languages in order to *stop* living with them, does this not mean infinitely to multiply our words and to extend our silence by as much?

The end is always the beginning of an endless destruction.

No longer to work at revolution, no longer to say freedom, hate, love. To be the book against the book as it comes into being, haunted by the last—the first—book. To be freedom. To be revolution.

Here, the *dawn of the book* reveals a universe in ashes at the heart of the universe, as the desert *speaks the bloody dawn of what has been: but how come we can still hear the voice, fresh, at the end of time in the condemned word?*

"Outside the gap."

Claude Royet-Journoud

". . . all a writer admits is writing."

Jean Catesson
(*Critique* no. 357, February 1977)

"Writing is ungraspable future."

Rosmarie Waldrop

". . . anonymous and changing like duration."

Joseph Guglielmi

"Contemporary across millennia."

Didier Cahen

What is illegible *outside* becomes legible *within*.

To turn the outside in, and the inside out, is what writers stubbornly attempt.

Perhaps writing only shows openings into the possible.

Leave it to God to die of God where He is silent.

The Setting   The Opening

"This new opening of a site"

This is what Anne-Marie Albiach, with exemplary lucidity, allows us to live.

We can no longer escape the boundlessness that makes our boundaries tremble.

A trembling in turn overcome by the push toward an unknown that fascinates each of the words we are riveted to.

"shift from one to another setting"

The setting being the opening that is "inaccessible and only reconcilable," as the horizon is to the horizon.[1]

1. Quotations are from *Etat,* translated by Keith Waldrop, Windsor, Vt.: Awede Press, 1989.

May He Rest in *Thus*

"*then*

               For THUS is dead

to descend

behind the sandy

               May He rest in THUS."

Thus, Roger Giroux is no more. He foundered in the book, and the book is no ordinary grave: book protected from whiteness, from the snows of pure consciousness and death.

"searching for this   in the unpublishable distance   I"

Thus, a poet spoke and fell silent. An immense silence has fallen over the simplest words that brought him their shattered portions of silence, of the sea, perhaps, where books are made and unmade.

"and the single
act
of choosing

for the dark paper gulls"

Thus, there was his attempt to lift, from sea to inaccessible mountain top, an emptiness laden with all the weight of trees.

"*First page (it snows) in the heart of a tree by the ocean*"

"and a few trees
scot-free

over the void of gesture"

Thus, there was this gesture and this single tree by the ocean, whose fruit we loved before it was engulfed.

Thus, nothing now: but, with this nothing, all that had managed to come out of words and is now returned to words; all that had once been able to come out of his heart and has now stopped beating with his heart, on the last page of the book.

We shall never leave the mountain tops, nor the sea, while listening to death.
We shall never leave the tree nor the question of death.

"I was the object of a question outside my line of duty. It was there, but did not insist, called my name gently so as not to scare me. But I had no way of keeping track of the sound of its voice. So I called it absence. . ."

Thus, a book. on the scale of the void, to contain the starry void—O night—of an unforgettable poet.

Writing in Motion
(Short Reply to a Questionnaire of *La Quinzaine Littéraire:* Does Writing Have a Gender?)

What sets writing in motion? Writing itself, and we are riveted to it.

In creativity, now the feminine element dominates, now the masculine.

Within us they are, however, fused to such a degree that we cannot sort them out.

Once written, the book comes free of the author.

It is perhaps at this moment, when the latter finds himself without words, that he could responsibly try to answer the question posed by your paper; but then it is also too late.

1977
(Reply to a Questionnaire of *Les Nouvelles Littéraires*)

There are limits to despair.
There are no limits to hope.

What counts most out of a year just past? What memory? What event?

So much has been said; so much left unsaid. The future cares only about the future.

What lasts? Perhaps a gesture. Perhaps a child's word or an adult's.

To remain open. No doubt it is on preserving this openness, so difficult to defend, that our capacity for astonishment depends. A capacity that makes the world seem ever new.

But what world are we speaking of? There are no more open eyes just as there are no more bright stars since a yellow star marked innumerable innocents for death, since base violence and torture shamelessly defied the light of day.

No word but has issued from silence. The heavier the silence, the graver the word.

In this eleventh month of the year, a silence charged with intense emotion has suddenly come to stop all words, interrupt all talk.

This silence has been imposed on the world for a few moments by a man, by the Egyptian head of state, who has offered to share it with his enemies of yesterday, knowing that this silence contains the torture of millions of people and also contains their hopes.

Has this silence not always been ours, the silence of our deserts? As if all we try to say could only be said through it?

Then there was the smile, the handshake, the exchange of words unsure of their future, marked by our expectation of the word we wanted to hear, which could only be announced by a confusion of words glad to prepare its way.

Nobody has done more than this man to give a chance to the outstanding, clinching word that presides over our actions.

For this word, first and last, we are listening with suspense.

The Invention of the Word

In the wake of a book already old, yet still present. In the wake of a book's cry of pain.

Who speaks dies of speaking. His death is a saying *in itself*.

We never cease to die of this saying:

"He told me:
My race is yellow.
I answered:
I'm of your race.

He told me:
My race is black.
I answered:
I'm of your race.

He told me:
My race is white.
I answered:
I'm of your race,

for my sun was the yellow star,
for I am wrapped in night,
for my soul, like the tables of the law,
is white."

Which law do you mean? The law has no memory: memory, no law.

Do not try to remember. You are yourself remembrance. Did I say I remembered?

All invention originates in words. We are their tributaries. They mark us as strongly as we mark them. Words for joy. Words for misery. Words for indifference and for hope. Words for things and for people. Words for the universe and for the void.

And behind each of them: life, simple or complex, with death in ambush.

Invention in turn invents us. Uses us for its own ends. Distances us from others or brings us closer. Celebrates or attacks us. Helps us or knocks us down and takes the place of the law.

But which invention do you mean here? The invention of a word, of course. A custom-made word, made to fit its deadly invention: APARTHEID.

A for Abasement
P for Police
A for Affront
R for Regulation
T for Treachery
H for Hegemony
E for Emasculate
I for Intolerance
D for Distress, immense distress of a people.

"For my birthday," said a white South African, "I told a friend I would 'have' a negro. I kept my word."

True, the courts of his country sentenced him to two months imprisonment, with *suspended sentence.*

Remorseless reprobates with suspended sentences, a word of unsuspected power weighs on you with all the weight of your victims. A word which your conscience tries in vain to abolish: the word MEMORY.

To this word you will succumb.

(Text written for an anthology against Apartheid published by UNESCO in 1983.)

Will the unacceptable become part of the acceptable?
The void is irrigated with blood.

The Wall

"Absent wherever an absent man is celebrated."
René Char

"On both sides of the wall, we have vainly labored to shield our common speech against its intolerable solitude," he said, forgetting that, jointly, we return it to this solitude.

"These walls that all say *here, now*."

"No wall for relief. No wall but flaunts a refusal."

"Wavering boundary of a wall, denied or reinforced, hated, hoped for as if *being there* meant above all to hesitate between being stifled and dissolving into space."

Marcel Cohen
(Murs)

"Your ink has learned
the violence of the wall."
Paul Auster
(Unearth)

"I cover the walls with words that make them invulnerable"

Jacques Dupin
(L'embrasure)

"No wall; no more silence. We have all bet on a silence from beyond."

Marcel Cohen
(Murs)

To each tear its own walls. The height of the wall measures our dead pain.

The blood of the wall is cement: rich, hardened blood.

The talk between stone and stone is of plaster—or dust.

Stone is more eloquent than the road.

Only what is not the book, but the stone of the book; not the stone, but the transparency of the book; not the transparency, but the far side of the horizon of the book, can hear the silence.

Of this silence, where the wound has not stopped bleeding and will never run dry, Marcel Cohen has tried to write, at the price of a dawn, for the benefit of a starry night.

Dazzled. Blind. Crushed.

Do not look either in front or behind, but within yourself. There is the point of departure.

There is room for only one pain at a time: one book.

Stone is heavy with all the contained patience of death.

At which unknown, stormy limits of the mind, of life, appears the solar smile of the eternal pariah?
Rainbow. Rainbow.

So many tears tinted by the light, counted by the night.

"If you drive a nail into a wall you are only filling a hole," he said.

The power of thought holds sway above our chasms. Do not be deceived by their likeness. You will not recognize yours.

Questions are the downbeat of dialogue; answers, its weak upbeat.
Out of this weakness questions are born.

> ("I persist, but with a foreboding that tiredness is inherent in my very hope, that the brighter world which, the border once crossed, could be mine forever, is every day more menaced."
>
> Marcel Cohen
> (Miroirs)

> First flight, then fissures, nowhere any anchor. Never any peaceful abandon.)

Can we separate sky from sky?
Or sand from sand:
the grain of sand in the sky,
the sky in the grain of sand.
Infinite alliance.

> "Only the eyes are still able to utter a scream."
> René Char

"Ashes, all that faces up."

Didier Cahen

"du sollst nicht
aufsehn zum Himmel, du liessest
ihn denn, wie er dich,
im Stich, neben-
lichtig."

Paul Celan
(*Schneepart*)

"We can only live in what is ajar, exactly on the dividing line of dark and light. But we are irresistibly hurled onward, our whole person aiding the vertiginous push."

"Truth needs two faces: one for our trip there, the other for our return."

René Char

"The well of truth is an aesthetics all by itself."

Max Jacob
(Letter to EJ)

"The idea is never limpid enough. The researcher throws so much light on it that finally the thing is blinded by words."

George Auclair
(*Le même et l'autre*)

Memory of Paul Celan

That day. The last. Paul Celan at my house. Sitting in this chair that I have right now been staring at for a long time.

Exchange of words, closeness. His voice? Soft, most of the time. And yet it is not his voice I hear today, but his silence. It is not him I see, but emptiness, perhaps because, on that day, each of us had unawares and cruelly revolved around himself.

The Man with the Secret
(Max Jacob)

1

"It is syntax that reveals the individual."

"To work out a theory you must try to know yourself, and this effort is good.

"Truly red hot work is work on yourself."

"Theory is a corset, a bridge, individuality."

"The word is much, but the sentence carries the emotion."

Max Jacob
(Letter to EJ)

"I too have known these funerals. If I could, I would start all over, but death will not leave me the time."

Max Jacob
(Letter to EJ)

"Wakeful at night, wakeful at night. In the silver rays of the night."

Max Jacob
("Rivage")

My last message, sent in February 1944 to Max Jacob through the Apostolic Delegation of Cairo where I lived—twenty-five words of worry and affection—was returned to me with the word "deceased" on the back.

What remains is the future
Not the present with its grief.

Max's future is today. It has been every day for thirty years. It will be tomorrow for a long time to come. For his work continues to hold us, and largely by the very quality that escaped the best of his contemporaries, the playful gravity.

"Voices have told me *na*, which means *secret* in Hebrew," he had written in *Défense de Tartufe*.

The man with the secret, not with the legend. Max Jacob, even while cultivating his legend, was bent on piercing the mystery of an existence pledged to heaven and hell.

There is always a world beyond—or below—lived or to be lived, even in his least significant phrases. Poetry transfigures them. Poetry, the permanent mystery into which all mysteries enter.

Out and out extravagances fed by his humor, disarming excesses in or out of control, so many crests on the horizon. No doubt, a difficult road toward God. For God (who became the focus of his meditations after the famous night when Christ appeared to the poet) is also the step that precedes the step on the road.

To place himself in relation to God and to language was his constant care.

He wrote for Marcoussis's benefit: "We are inexpressible, inexpressive fellows and I hope you will manage to express yourself in something . . . which will hardly express you, but will, with luck, express something that is not you, yet expresses something of you."

Inherent in the given possibility of speech is the impossibility of expressing ourselves.

To express, with luck, something that is not us, yet expresses something of us, is the aim of all creation and is revealed by the work.

Obsessed by suicide—had he not written as early as 1919: "Quarrels, my ever more insatiable pride, all the intoxications cannot silence the secret and haunting idea of suicide"?—and as if he must constantly redeem himself by destroying himself, he went toward the death decreed by the yellow star sewn on his coat. A death glimpsed many times.

"We must expect, in the course of centuries, to rejoin martyrdom that makes blood fruitful. As for me, I have long been ready for it both as a Jew and a fervent Catholic," he wrote me in January 1939 and, in a last letter dated May 1: "I am out of the world. I can only suffer martyrdom."

Thus, in examined faith, remorse, pain, and wonder, from book to book and even to the silence of all Words, was fulfilled his accepted, his invented life.

Perhaps it is at the edge of this silence that we have always had to read him.

"I thank you for having been born of the suffering Jewish race. For only he who suffers and knows he suffers and offers his suffering up to God, is saved. You made me suffer from my stifled, abominable childhood on—in this already humiliated race—and if You did not make me conscious of it then, You reserved for me the power one day to offer You this contribution to my salvation."

Max Jacob
Méditations religieuses,
September 1941,
8:10 A.M.

3

"Never before was death so smooth in death. Never before were we so alike," Sarah had said.

"For us, death was the transparency of death," Yukel had replied.

"A look too wide to hold."

Rosmarie Waldrop

"We should learn to write only on days of courage and strength."

Georges Auclair
(Le même et l'autre)

"Sand, sand, life. Appeased blood, oblivious of its past efforts, breeze, smell of water, life."

Marcel Cohen
(Galpa)

"When the caresses have gone, there remains immense violence."

Paul Eluard

154

Days of Wrinkles

"Humankind is becoming aware of itself. We should talk to it in its language, and the poet is the one to talk to it with grandeur."

Max Jacob
(Letter to EJ)

I

"Simply to take my stand on a plain truth, that is
to say, one that rests on a single cutting edge."

Antonin Artaud

(Le Pèse-nerfs)

The Infallible Decree
(Jacket copy for *L'Arrêt de mort* by Maurice
Blanchot, Collection "L'Imaginaire," Gallimard)

No book has ever been to this degree a testing ground of
its law. Sovereign gravity of *L'Arrêt de mort!* The implacable
Death Sentence, the infallible decree comes down like a knife
on each of its pages, not to separate the story into two almost
equal parts, but, on the contrary, to mark with a cut (and at
least once it's a cut of the most visible kind) the passage from
one to the other, from life to death, the better to fuse them
afterwards.

From now on books will be divided into those written before *L'Arrêt,* which circle it, afraid and yet fascinated, and
those written after it—or at the same time?—which accept,
assimilate, or, rather, apply it. In the image, perhaps, of what
has, after "this deep hatchet cut" dug into the middle of J's
palm. . . . "And if this line is called the line of fortune, I must
say it made fortune look tragic."

The law is the eye of death. Three characters—with one
single uncontrollable passion—will live and die of the infinite
humanity and glacial cruelty of its glance; will, surrounded by
occasional witnesses who make the story plausible, live the
death of the other and die their own death.

Law of the universe and of the book. "What happened had
happened long before." And what are these words of death
that are not at all silence? "The extraordinary begins the moment I stop."

("If the other warrants my responsibility toward him, I warrant that he will leave a trace. This modifies my relation to the world because, enlisted in a future whose gravity I know in advance, my only support is his pledge to respect our pact to the letter.

"Thus he alone can certify my good faith, as no one beside me could testify to his," he had written.

"You oppose me to my freedom in the name of a solidarity which is our road to freedom.

"There is the contradiction," he said.

Perhaps "I" only affirms "You"—confirms the "I" with the "You," its counterpart and parity.

The trace is whiter where scrutinized.

"The reality of the 'I' is the subtle fruit of an imaginary 'You.'

"Its naive projection," he had noted.

Absence has woven our bond: which binds Nothing to Nothing.

Not to have a face, so that God alone can see it. All doors are of this earth.)

There Is No Trace But in the Desert
With Emmanuel Lévinas

1

I know he exists. I see him. I touch him. But who is he and who am I? We know, one and the other, one for the other. On this basis . . .

This face, perhaps of a face forgotten and regained.—Mine before mine? Or after?

What this voice says, which is perhaps only the voice of unsayable sayings telling its misfortunes, hence saying nothing.

The emptiness of what is said where it gets lost, where we get lost.

And yet . . .

A passive, though gnawing absence.

There is no trace but in the desert, no voice but in the desert.

The beginning of action is passage, wandering.

From the unsayable to the unsayable.

Leaving familiar, known sites—landscapes, faces—for an unknown place—the desert, the new face, the mirage?

The infinite face of Nothing, with its weight of Nothing, of all faces reduced to a single one, mine, and lost.

And passage?—Perhaps what has neither end nor beginning, unfixed trace, non-trace of a burning trace; raw sensibility of sand and skin in their extremity.

On skin, the trace, and in the heart.

Perhaps this trace approaches the face, approach always delayed, revealed. What carries us to the infinite.

What beats in our chests.

Then rhythm would be intuiting the trace. We would be the trace.

If I am the trace, I can only be so for another. But if the other is yet another—otherness to yet others—who will notice the trace? Perhaps others are the abyss of the trace.

Thought in infinite regress, writing of the abyss. At the edge. But if the trace is in me, flows, beats within me? Every impulse of my body is a recorded, counted trace, multiplied by fever—by love, pain, delirium. The trace is tied to being, to essence, as to the emptiness with which it perhaps resonates.

2

Of this trace, a face. Which? Everything—and nothing—is in the face, in the effaced face that is reborn of its effacement, that rises out of the emptiness of its traits forgotten, lost, and restored by death. As if death knew it, knew all faces with their particularities and their leveling banality, the test of likeness. With their names: faces of pronounceable or unpronounceable names.

This obsession with faces become face itself, obsessive trace of passage, passage that takes the form of a face, models its traits. Witness face, mute, garrulous, listened to, blamed.

A name is no doubt a trace. But whose name? A name as name, as vocable. A name as impossible proof.

A face asleep, a face waking, some trace of dark or light.

To step on a trace means stepping on a face.

We should, on these paths, walk on our mouths, advance on our lips to kiss the trace. Love rules the road.

But is there any road without a trace?

Yesterday is the trace of tomorrow, but tomorrow wants to be without trace, virgin or, rather, would like to be its own trace heralding its advent, anticipated by our expectation. Then yesterday would be the promise of a trace always still to come. Then the trace would be marked from day after to day after, a trace of the future. What happens would be what in some way has already left traces at the heart of our daily expectations and hopes, tracing the outline of hope, of hope as a trace. And also fear, because death is both the trace we dread and the loss of all trace.

And the face? Perhaps it is what is given as universal, human, divine trace, as reason—motive—for passage and as figure of its indestructible absence, as what lights up and goes out in the face of the other become night and morning of his ungraspable face, the absolute otherness of any face.

Turned back into nothing, but also a mirror of Nothingness, a reflection of its broken mirror, its oval broken in reflected distance.

Could it be that death is the only trace? But how would it be marked? Not only would it not be marked, but, on the contrary, it would escape all established traces. It would even present itself as this escape, as its shore and crest, with the ocean roaring and the wind blowing to deafen the nonexistent trace, to hound it down and mark it in salt or knock it out with immense breath; as if it had been noticed and grasped in its dazzling negation, its inviolable transparency.

3

At these limits, what desire would dare declare itself desire, unless infinite desire, the untouchable sky at the foot of which our desires died along with our limits, unless azure in love with the azure beyond horizons?

This tension toward another face as if come out of the clouds or the pure light of unsuspected heights; this blind attraction to a distant, blinding face, these contractions of our features at the real or imagined approach of other features, like ours in their apparent difference; this repressed appeal, held back to the point where it is but need, desire, hope of an appeal among all appeals, all encounters, and all rejections; this outcry, this small noise, this commotion and confused contentment that menace us, hovering, and whose heirs or victims we are; this love of love, this pain of pain, this trace of a trace which would proclaim them by proclaiming itself, explain them by explaining itself? Perhaps this "third person" "beyond being" "who is not defined by the self?" But is it a matter of that? Unless this "third person," this third character, is death, absent reality whose name makes all reality founder in its name.

4

The Good—what is, first, good in itself for others and, in others, good for itself—this bond, this intimate, repressed, and flaunted solidarity, this announcement, this coming of a drawn, empty face, this distance stealing in, outlined against space, forming and unforming, this space gathered and momentarily folded in on itself so that it seems an image of what is without image and yet so regarded, so loved—What can be more intimate than a face? It glows as at the heart of faith, at the threshold and end of all proximity—, this imperceptible grazing of, we might say, leaf against leaf, this frail, light, airy contact of feverish nakedness with nakedness itself, this shedding of leaves evoking the natural misery of tree and book at their end; all this and also the seizure, the sudden shock, the fright and wonder in front of the unknown we have always known, but so buried in memory, so disfigured: Is this truth? Is it what we do not dare directly to call truth, so much does it escape us? Is it the unidentifiable face of truth through which our face reaches its truth, as if we had to visualize its invisible features on the model of our own to believe in it and, by and by, see it, though it be only the presentiment, ardent desire, and mad need we have of its presence—sublimated image—to which we are eternally committed like the blue of the sky to the blue of the sea? Face of the time before day, smooth and getting smoother with each showing, each short-lived— fatal—metamorphosis until the last, total, transparency?

5

God, as the absolute Other of others: as if we must first become familiar and share responsibility with other faces before we can approach through them the absolute Other without face. As if on all drowned faces there glowed the loss of His. As if His face had paid the loss of all of ours.

Here is distress, the despair of love within love, infinite pain within pain, delirium blazing within delirium. Here is passivity rent in its deep sovereignty. Here, like a bottomless cliff, like the dark of all nights.

How far does our responsibility go? The void is forged by our hands.

6

Then, the question.

The question means that, for the time of its formulation, we do not belong. We do not belong with belonging; we are unbound within bonds. Detached, in order to become more fully attached and then again detached. It means we forever turn the *inside out,* set it free, revel in its freedom, and die of it.

Cruel calling and recalling into question. Double responsibility.

I am. I become. I write. I write only in order to become. I am only the man I become who, in turn, stops being to become the other he has potentially always been. I am all the others I will be. I will not be. They will be me who cannot be.

The question leaves a blank: the page.

Writing is erased in writing. Black turns blank in the dark. The blank remains.

Blanks are contagious. Black opens into blank, which fills its opening. Blank duration.

What is said leaves no trace. It is always the already said, the trace stepped over—neglected?

To set out to discover the trace means perhaps to continue writing, to circle around the unfindable trace.

All traces of words are in the word.

Word: overload of nothing.

Alliance of step and trace. Does the trace come due with the step? Unless the step comes due with the trace.

. . . a step, like a well.

The question of the word, the question of the written, the question of the book are questions put to blankness, to emptiness, to the void.

Passage. The passing of a wise man, of wisdom—or a fool? A blank means passage into death.

The water of passage quenches our thirst for the unknown.

The unknown is our last passage, the most perilous. Death, in this sense, displaces the unknown.

Writing is perhaps only a way of dying of the words of our death; and a trace, only the progressive unveiling of a shadow, O ultimate blank.

Under this blank, we repose.

Under this immaterial blank face.

("The sky was only a little darker and higher."

René Daumal

"Never will the spirit dismiss the letter that re-veals it."

Emmanuel Lévinas

"All the great mystics of all religions would be ours if they had broken the yoke of their religion to the point where we could take it on."

". . . hence we idealize the tendency, in every instant, to call everything into question."

Roger Gilbert-Lecomte)

II

"I find it very difficult to know who I am. In this matter, others are better informed than I am. For a long time, I believed the opposite, for example, that an author knows himself better than the reader knows him. It is not so."

Jean Grenier

Is it not one of Jean Grenier's merits that he raised the question—without, however, raising it—of loyalty across the breach of a tie, of loyalty to the breach?

Detachment, too, has its bridges.

Extract from a Speech
(given on April 21, 1982, in Paris,
at the Foundation for French Judaism)

We violate a book in order to read it, but we offer it closed.

. . . For all my being bound to the French language, I know the place I occupy in the literature of our country is not strictly speaking a place. It is not so much the place of a writer as of a book that does not fit any category. A place defined, then, by the book and immediately claimed by the book to follow. Place of writing vacated by what is written, as if every page of the book let us occupy it only to give access to the next page, as if the book made and unmade itself in an appropriated space which, once covered with words, becomes the space of the book.

And it is the same way within the large movement that has carried my works to their illusory completion.

There is no center. There is a point that engenders another point around which an eccentric utterance establishes itself, an interrogation develops. It is the point of no return.

This absence of place, as it were, I claim as my own. It confirms that the book is my only habitat, the first and also the final. Place of a vaster non-place where I live.

A word emerges from the silence of all the others, and this silence is also the desert.

If I had to define the words in my books, I would say they are words of the sands—of sand—made audible, visible for a brief instant, words of intense harkening and very ancient memory.

The experience of the desert is both the place of the Word—where it is supremely word—and the non-place where it loses itself in the infinite. So that we never know whether we catch it at the moment it springs up or at the moment it begins ever so slowly to fade: the dazzling moment of its issue or its imperceptible vanishing.

And perhaps all we can ever hear is a word near its death, because there is no beginning that has not known its end within it. As if the word, in order to be completely grasped, must also bear witness to its passage from birth to death: from the nothing its rise illumines to the nothing it rejoins in its fall.

In this case, to create means only to show the birth and death of an object. We speak, we write but for the moment. Duration is not for us.

The weight of words is certainly nothing but the weight of the experience of words across human experience, weight of a common past, and glimpse of a shared future.

It is obvious that certain words charged with all the feeling we are capable of, such as, for instance, the words "love" and "death," do not have the same resonance for all of us. For every life is unique. Our own story, the story of our days and nights, stands behind them with our joys and pains, our tears and our laughter. It is this story alone that the words we use (and whose prey we are) reveal through their very inability to hold it.

But how is it that in telling our life they also make us relive a story recorded within our own and older than we are?

To hear a word means to hear it especially in its echoes, its infinite prolongations. The book is built on listening for these.

I have always answered the question: "Do you consider yourself a Jewish writer?" with: "I am a writer and a Jew." An answer perhaps disconcerting at first, but which comes out of my great concern not to reduce either term to what I might be able to say about them jointly.

And yet it was in declaring myself a writer that I felt myself already Jewish. In the sense that the writer's history and the Jew's are both the history of the book they lay claim to.

It was my questioning as a writer that allowed me to approach Jewish questioning in all its gravity. As if the Jew's progress at a given moment became mere progress-into-writing.

Whether talmudist or cabbalist, the Jew's relation to the book is as fervent as that of the writer to his text. Both have the same thirst to learn, to know, to decipher their fate carved into every letter from which God has withdrawn. And what matter if their truth differs. It is the truth of their being. It is the truth of their language. Word of two books in one. For the Jewish writer is not necessarily the one who privileges the word "Jew" in his writings, but the one for whom the word "Jew" is contained in all the words of the dictionary, a word the more absent for being, by itself, every one of them.

The word "Jew" is born and dies with every Jew, word of an immemorial wound renewed at every moment.

Six million burned bodies divide our century in two with the horrible image they perpetuate.

Who could ever measure the extent of suffering that has forgotten even its origin in order to remember only its innocence?

No, a Jewish theme is not enough to make a book Jewish. The Jewish tale is much less in the anecdote, the confession, the local color, than in the writing. You cannot tell Auschwitz. Every word tells it to us.

There is such a thing as Jewish writing, disturbing for having always managed to survive. Writing within the writing it inhabits. You recognize it by its stubborn resolve to find expedients, to question itself, to go over and over the unsayable. Vertiginous discourse straining toward a future whose brittleness it knows from the start. Words of anxiety, alarming but brotherly, beyond trials, beyond their own *communication*.

Bound to the text, the Jew facing his own truth lives, by

conscientiously repeating every word, the hope and distress of the one word he has made his name.

The Jewish word is word of the abyss the book opens onto.

The Jew and the writer experience the same perpetual beginning—which is not a re-beginning—the same amazement at what is written, the same faith in what remains still to be read and said. God is His word, and this living word must forever be rewritten. The believing Jew cannot go toward God except through the Book. But his commentary on the original Text is not a commentary on the divine Word, only on human words dazzled by the latter like moths by the lamp. It annotates the frenzy of the moth, not the blinding light. The fate of insect and book is to perish burning, but they do not die in the same way nor in the same space of time. Many are the approaches to the text, and often mysterious. The roads of the book are roads of instinct, listening, attention, reserve, and daring laid out by words and sustained by questions. Roads toward the open.

Could a truth, which is not felt each time as a new truth, claim to be the only truth? God dwells in eternity, man in a life headed toward death which our thoughts try to sound. Word of immortality against all finite words. The book bears witness to this conflict that no page can resolve. And yet God lives only in the words of man, who is inspired and destroyed by them. Shared torment.

Could the most authentic religious utterance be that of the atheist? We do not truly speak except at a distance. There is no word not severed. This separation is the unbearable absence every word butts up against, as any given name does against the unpronounceable divine Name.

And yet, separate in order to be recognized—for do we not need the blank space, the fraction of silence between words to read or hear them?—the words have no tie to one another except this absence.

I have tried in my work to make perceptible the movement

words follow, from the silence before, which they break, to the silence they introduce as they hush. Infinite of the book.

My work (I always quail to call it that) has often been said to be subversive. If it has appeared so, it is simply because, tormented by my uncertainties and determined to overcome them, I have shamelessly and without hesitation exhibited my contradictions.

Contradictions upset, irritate even, because they undermine judgment.

Once out of our mouth, the word is in exile. Identifying with it means embracing our future.

Why is the cry of the newborn infant pushed out of the womb a cry of pain? No doubt because, in asserting itself in its own language, a cry of life, it is already a cry of exile.

Through our words we are forever this cry of an infant in search of a familiar face, of a warm breast, of love.

Like a star in the night, a word is exiled at the heart of the blank page. All words participate in this exile.

We ask questions only of exile, of absence. We write nothing else.

If an answer establishes its place, a question makes that place its universe. There is no place for questions which is not also a question of place. Answers mean sleep, death. Waking means questioning. In privileging the latter I have, not without effort, preserved openness. There has never been a place for me which was not also an opening out from the place.

Thus have I lived the book.

I have wanted to push as far as possible, which for me means to the boundary of the sayable, the gradual adjustment of the Jew I am and the book I carry in me. But which Jew am I talking about and which book? Perhaps about neither, but about being faithful to a word from the desert, which the Jew made his own because it had come out of all our crumbled words, and about being faithful to an absolute, mythical book, which every book tries in vain to reproduce.

Our relation to Jewishness, to writing, is a relation to strangeness both in its primitive sense and the one it has acquired since. It can turn us, at the heart of our un-condition, into a stranger among strangers.

Identity is perhaps a trap. We are what we become.

Then, being a Jew and a writer would mean taking on simultaneously the unsurpassed fullness of a Jewish beyond and the beyond of a book.

And the boldest challenge would be, at each step, to find the secret measure of the incommensurability of any relation to the absolute.

In the short run, impossible means failure to go beyond. Refusing this failure may transform the impossible into adventurous possibility.

Here is our freedom.

I would like to end with three quotations:

First, from Emmanuel Lévinas: "*If you question your Jewish identity, you have already lost it, yet are holding on to it still, since otherwise you could avoid the question.*"

Then, from Maurice Blanchot: "*Who writes is in exile from writing. That is his own country, in which he is no prophet.*"

And finally one borrowed from one of the imaginary characters of my books behind whom I shelter: "*Faced with the impossibility of writing that paralyzes every writer and the impossibility of being Jewish, which has for two thousand years racked the people of this name, the writer chooses to write, and the Jew to survive.*"

("In the eyes of Judaism, there is certainly a pro-
fane area that must be penetrated by sainthood."
Gershom Scholem
(*Fidelité et utopie,*
trans. Marguerite Delmotte
and Bernard Dupuy)

"The strength of Judaism," he said, "is to pro-
voke contradictions in the name of the One Truth."
And added: "For truth, every day is a mirror of
victory.")

Extract from a Speech
(given on the occasion of a day in honor of P. P. Pasolini, Milan, May 2, 1983)

What ties one writer to another lies beyond praise, in the most intimate and most silent part of their being. That is the site of their closeness, at the heart of an adventure that annuls their differences.

This is why, tarrying for a moment in this place of friendship where word echoes word, I would like to be paradoxical and evoke silence: the silence in which are buried the words of a life and death the book can give back to us.

The book whose vocation is, certainly, to occasion countless readings, but whose mystery bursts open for only one reader at a time, for *its* reader. Crossroads of privileged encounters, the book can affirm itself only by multiplying, but any occasional or familiar decipherer can all by himself force its destiny.

The writer is his book. But we do not all enter it through the same door. Rather, it is always through ourselves that we approach a writer. Our desire to resemble him makes him our creature, for we unconsciously lend him our own traits. He is our other self, not by his will, but ours. Hence, when we venture to speak of him we never know if we are not, finally, speaking of ourselves.

Our speeches here, today, honor a strong, absent personality: a writer, filmmaker, pamphleteer, thinker, militant; a poet, finally—a poet in all senses of the term, a great poet because he paid with his very life for discovering a sound, a vocabulary, a phrasing, a song—whether of joy, revolt, or distress—an image, a silence. He knew that poetry is an act of total commitment, that what it says—without really saying it, saying it obliquely—is but the risk taken by a man who wants to make the poem's words his own.

In his quest for the absolute, *toward* an absolute that haunted him day and night, Pasolini explored all roads open to him, roads of the possible and impossible, up to the one he knew was fatal, of which his tragic death gives us a glimpse.

He carried to the highest level his inquiry into man and his language, denouncing all that blocked his path and suddenly seemed the insolent challenge, the intolerable obstacle he could only destroy by destroying himself.

Nobody burned with a stronger flame for man and his truth, which perhaps is but the love a man bears his neighbor and the truth.

The answer lies in the question it conveys.

The Word of the Book

Book answers to book.

My friendship with Roger Caillois was based on writing. First, a brief encounter in Cairo, twenty-five years ago. Mutual but guarded sympathy. I was suspicious and ill at ease. He likewise. I had not concealed the fact that I had reservations about some of his books and had read and rejected others with irritation. He appreciated my frankness. He could not stand compromise.

I had taken a few timid steps in his work, and he had come to meet me. I told him that I had probably read him poorly. We parted as friends.

Then I left Egypt and settled in Paris. This was in 1957. He was traveling much of the time. I saw him once or twice. I told him that, contrary to what the critics thought—at least judging by what articles I had seen—the very diversity of his questioning showed profound concern and anxiety. And that his work, wilfully haughty and distant—I knew his predilection for works "written at a distance"—might well turn out to be among the most tormented of our time for all that it does not say, or admits only grudgingly, here and there. Later, reading *Cases d'un échiquier* confirmed me in my opinion.

I also remember talking about his obsession with death, how one could discover the fascination it held for him in most of his texts.

For my part, after publishing a large collection of poems and aphorisms in 1959, I set out on a different road, on a stubborn, page by page questioning of origins and the book, to which—as well as to its form and writing—he was responsive from the start.

Examination abolishes limits. At the extreme boundary, the book tortured by the question is written.

Can we question death?—We question nothing else.

In that case, writing would mean accepting or, rather, *seeking* a permanent confrontation with death.

Moreover, can questioning be a bond? Questioning which, born of doubt, always challenges and delivers us, empty-handed, to death?

For the two of us, it presided over our relationship.

The unsayable lies at rock bottom of what is said. We navigate on the surface: even, smooth, transparent, or opaque surfaces; but never level.

Silence and death—unexplorable depth—cannot be expressed directly. They can only, O paradox, be translated, exposed through the insidious bias of their opposite.

Thus we are made to *hear* silence, to *live* death.

Thus the sensuous, smooth unfolding of waves reveals, no less than the stormy clash of their crests and valleys, the churning fullness of the sea. Thus, when we closely examine an object cramped in its boundaries, it gradually leads us to the confines of the invisible, whence it emerges, metamorphosed.

The mystery Roger Caillois has always sought to explore—"I have, however, always taken care to preserve a portion of mystery whose origin I tracked in vain"—may not, as we would like to believe, lie in beings or in things, but at the extremes, where they no longer count.

From death to death, from silence to silence, a book is a milestone, never the end.

Never the end, but the priming of an expected, almost hoped-for, end; secretly hoped for, because inventing an end to an adventure staked out with risks is a pledge of future rest, a chance to withdraw with dignity.

The writer knows by instinct that he can only fail in his mad enterprise of setting himself to words—like setting oneself to listen, to dress, to die—but he pretends not to know or, rather, miraculously stops being convinced of it the moment he takes up his pen. For we cannot persevere in a task unless we believe in it. Is it not in *Approches de l'imaginaire* that Roger Caillois notes: "I have learned that, whatever I undertake, I can do nothing but persevere"?

A work may be the fruit of daring, but it is first of all an act of faith, an intimate need, a vital necessity to forget, through which the writer regains his initial availability and with it his freedom to create.

Failure is transformed into victory and trembles to be unmasked.

For an artist, to fail is not just being doomed not to succeed, but also, as for a ship, to crash into the shore or, incapable of further effort, to suffer the humiliation of being towed to shore.

To these various, all in all pathetic and not very enviable ends, Roger Caillois opposes that of *Le Fleuve Alphée,* all refusal, stubbornness, and loyal love.

Can we save only what we master?

Mastery was Roger Caillois's chief concern. Lucid to the point of defiance.

Riveted to writing, which he worked hard to keep from the abyss where it might drown, perhaps after having discovered that the abyss was within.

If he had such a passion for stones it was because they carry writing from beyond time.

Also, they alone have bracketed both their dark existence and their blinding emptiness—as Caillois himself would try to do in one of his last books: "In this work, the word *bracket* designates the near-total of my life."

Countless, eternal stones that, inside their unechoing name, have already traveled all roads, climbed all peaks, rolled down all slopes before offering themselves to our curiosity and meditation.

Stones of marvels, of wounds, of secrets.

A friendship on the basis of books is at the same time the least possessive and the most intransigent. Least possessive because built on our differences, on full acceptance of the inevitable aggravation of these differences: path within the path, or virgin path veering off the path's edge. Most intransigent because constantly, entirely, threatened by each page, each word of the book.

But perhaps all books are simply written expression of a friendship searching for itself in the friendship of a stranger become our double: adversary and accomplice.

All brackets have, for infinite background, the void, and this void is still the book.

Remains the man whose affectionate presence has always delighted me.

Rereading this text (destined, with others, for the *Nouvelle Revue Française*'s homage to Roger Caillois) I notice that I have neither written a eulogy to his glory nor tried to encompass a work that I have long been familiar with. I have simply assembled some reflections, often interrogative, in the wake of a suspended, vaster interrogation: words of a vigilant closeness shared, now, in the shadow of a voice fallen silent.

> (*"To save time . . . that is my great purpose."*
> *"Great calm comes out of a multiplicity of occupations and fatigue.*
> *"Not to think of ourselves, to pursue an enterprise, to aim at a goal.*

"We find our center in the eye of the storm. Otherwise we are blown away.

"Those grains of sand we call 'I' pile up only because of the speed of their shifting.

"I define myself only by the end I tend toward—and this 'I' itself is only tension."

Jean Grenier
(Interview with Louis Foucher)

The Naked Sword
(Michel Leiris)

Silent sword. Silent nakedness. All silence wields a sword, all nakedness, its wound.

Silence of the *I* within its infinite utterances.

In this "terrain of truth," death is the judge.

Sentence. The text is nothing but the implacable sentence that no one escapes.

Writer and reader are lost in the same vocabulary.

And the earth bursts open, and horizons fuse.

It is language that creates risk.

"No matter how accustomed I am to observing myself, no matter how maniacal my taste for this bitter kind of contemplation, there are no doubt things that escape me, and probably the most obvious. Perspective is everything, and my portrait painted from my own perspective has every chance to leave in the dark certain details that for others must be the most flagrant," notes Michel Leiris.

Mouth of darkness! Sword over the entrance to the abyss. The never-yet-said, the unsayable. Would we take on the Void? We cannot fight absence. And yet the combat is within, in the wrinkles of emptiness: wrinkle against wrinkle, hollow against hollow.

The never-yet-said: is that the hollow? The unsayable, the ungraspable wrinkle? Fine, parallel lines, limpid your prolongations.

We let ourselves be carried along on nothing, in tow to Nothingness. Passage between words, between waters, but not stirring them, arousing only relative interest.

To speak for ourselves, to ourselves. To tell, tell of ourselves. A force out of control that suddenly heaves up the calm sea.

Do questions and answers not come out of a mad desire to know ourselves, a relentless determination to knock down the walls around us in the hope finally to win out over silence—as if we could, with our voices alone, fill the abyss?

"Since we have been in dialogue . . ." writes Hölderlin.

A verse on which Hegel meditates and comments:

"In the case in question," he states, "in order to be really, truly *man* and know himself as such, man must impose his idea of himself on others. He must make himself be recognized by others (in the extreme, ideal case, by all others)."

So the other is our mirror, judge, sentence, sword.

Is there no possible shelter for the word? It is fully itself only when *exposed*.

It can measure itself only against the word of the other, which it challenges.

Then, is writing for oneself really writing? Speaking for oneself, really speaking? True, nobody is alone with himself, and talking to oneself, after all, only multiplies, innocently, the story of one's life and death, starting from zero to repeat the smallest details of the same story for the benefit, each time, of a different self. A means, in short, to count our selves, to recount ourselves.

Does the book not always open to an unknown reader's curiosity?

Making this dialogue public means taking on all the risk inherent in all writing, all speech.

We have been read, been heard. We can no longer dodge judgment. No matter what the sentence, our awareness from now on depends on it.

The weight of our words is never more than that of their portion of the world.

So the text remains without object; the word, without echo, for the time of their retreat. The future plays on the other side of the river, in the sun.

The sea swallows all sounds, all calls, all screams that do not clear it. The anonymous companion from foreign parts has the grave privilege of bridging the distance that the book keeps from itself. For the book does not seek refuge outside its words, but in them, hiding in their heart of hearts. So that the book always leads to a book that remains to be discovered.

Like thought, truth—or what we take for it—is not the fruit of a coupling, but, on the contrary, of a rude grappling with an ambitious, arrogant, hostile truth or thought in constant motion—the more dizzying for being visible only in the light of its imperceptible, sudden displacements.

If we had no fear of this inevitable grappling, of the cruel and decisive confrontation with the *other*, would autobiography not quickly (in spite of the author's instinctive reticence) turn into some exercise of complacency?

It is always the *other* we come up against. Madness is perhaps only a dumb resolution to eliminate the other in the name of a unique word, free of people or world.

The word is twofold. At the heart of this duality, it is tested.

Every text, every discourse, witnesses the final triumph of the *other*. He will always lord it over us, and we probably write to escape his irksome sway. From this perspective, we might consider writing as an act of liberation, but it liberates the writer only to subject him the more.

So without the *other*, there is no end, no coming due. We collapse, each time, at his feet, unable to pursue further an adventure that is beyond us, unable to sustain a thought, a discourse too vast to be completed in harmony, to lead to some universal conclusion, which would never be more than the painful incompletion, the tragic and fatal inconclusiveness, of all works.

No departure where there can be no arrival. Neither time foreseen nor unforeseeable duration, the journey canceled.

We can only be read in time. The time of writing is a time outside time, but absorbed and so made legible by time.

And the intimate journal, whose aim is to elude time in order precisely to preserve words outside time, would it not in this perspective be the supreme attempt to escape the *other*?

And how define its limits when they are always those of a strength folded in on itself?

The word, in itself, is but a hole.

True dialogue unfolds in broad daylight: dialogue with the word, dialogue with our neighbor. It is the substance of autobiography in Michel Leiris's sense, and perpetuated by it. There, a man questions himself at the infinite edge of silence, where life and death take on their full meaning. Trickery is a shadow game, covert commerce. We are born and die at high noon.

The Unconditional, II
(Maurice Blanchot)

> A reflection at its peak, so unconditional that the words, relieved of the weight of their condition, regain a primal state of freedom.

Does the human condition disturb the unconditionality of God, as the limits of time disturb eternity, or the confines of space, the infinite?

God being divine unconditionally—a stranger to Himself precisely for being unaffected by His thoughts, unmarked by His acts—His attributes: eternal, infinite, just, good, wise, must escape all condition.

But what is Perfection, Justice, Goodness, or Wisdom if it remains untested, outside the time of trials?

What is eternity without time; the infinite, without limits? They can only be the ABSENCE they abut: absence that remains unconditionally absence, the inconceivable unconditional, absolute oblivion, oblivion that has forgotten and will plunge yet deeper into forgetting, death within death.

But what is death without the life it conditions, and vice versa? What is God without man, who limits Him by unlimiting himself?

Man's excess is an exemplary measuring of God.

Hence God's being beyond conditions depends on this first and ultimate evidence, the very condition of His freedom from them: *not to be*.

This is the unconditionality we come up against every time we espouse our condition or lack of it.

To be or not to be is the stake of a permanent conflict between condition and unconditon, presence and absence, and, further, between an absence conditioned by presence and unconditional absence that escapes all presence.

At which point of our presence do we become absent? At which point of our absence do we know we are present?

Does unconditionality come before or after conditions; absence before or after presence?

In other words, must we, in order to be present or absent, already have been absent or present?

If there is to be absence, there must have been a previous presence. But can there be presence without, at a given moment, there having been absence? In the first case, thought would come before the unthought; conditions, before the unconditional; limits, before the infinite; God, before and after God.

Then thought would have created God, Whom it created as the unthought.

This unthought *would have creative force.* It would lord it over thinking, would open thought onto itself and immolate it in its daring.

But if limit and thought come *first*, how can we imagine a limit without horizons, thought with only its own thoughts to think?

For this, we would have to conceive of a desolate universe, a transparent world. And if, by a miracle, we were to succeed, how could we help asking: what could limits be to transparency, what could thoughts be to the void, unless perhaps intimate torment and despair?

Is there such a thing as the condition (or lack of it) of being a stranger? Could it be that strangeness is unconditional, and its measure, the very divide that rejects it and that thought sets up?

From one end of death to the other, I am tempted to write. "Your letter does not interrupt the silence."

In other words, speech (which means presence, condition) cannot hope to move silence (which is unconditional); unconditional retreat of the word.

And what if the word itself were silence?

And what if silence were but fulfillment of an extreme word; as the invisible might well be the last stage of the visible?

God dies into God.

> *(The unconditional is not opposed to the neutral.*
> *It is its radical essence, condition of unconditional-*
> *ity, and unconditionality of all condition.*
>
> *It is the perfect condition of neutrality at the*
> *heart of unconditionality or of condition, of full life,*
> *of absolute place: it occupies the place that death*
> *occupies in life.)*

Louis-René des Forêts
or *The Unease of the Question*

"And now I expect you to ask me the question
that burns your lips."

(Le Bavard)

Which question is this? Perhaps the most obvious, raised
in each of Louis-René des Forêts's books. Question without
answer because it is difficult to pose, can only be posed in
terms of an already rejected answer, does not search for a
solution, knowing beforehand that there is none.

But first we must ask who is speaking where everything
speaks, where truth is a verbal explosion of the unstoppable
desire of words in love with their vertigo; as if it were more
urgent to say that we do not, ever, say anything, than to zero
in on this nothing.

Yet the stakes are greater.

Just as our insane need to overstep moves us to open freely
to existence, to take on all of it, it is a matter, somehow, of
yielding to the continuous displacement of words across time
and space, in order to die, not of each one, but of a death so
anonymous that it fuses with the void: the very void that
makes all reading possible.

Borne along by a "demented memory" that upsets all rec-
ollection, the word remembers only its intrepid forays into the
unknown and its inevitable failures of a weak word, always at
the mercy of its painful muteness. For it must, at all cost, leave
the silence that oppresses and risks stifling it.

Extravagant attempt to survive itself by rising up against all that annuls it, aware that it can succeed only by in turn anulling itself from within.

This annulment is perhaps what allows it to speak simply as a word; and its voluntary death is perhaps what assures its pure becoming.

But what is a word without the silence out of which it emerges?

We must bury the grain to have it bear fruit. Once it has blossomed, the days of its death are numbered.

This is why silence aims only to accompany the word to its fulfillment: silence sacrificed to a word that in turn gratifies it with a similar sacrifice, pays its debt with the same desperate gesture—as if only death could answer to death.

"In talking always, and always overbearingly, we glide toward the worst frivolity."[1]

Does gravity likewise pass through the frivolous—or what is taken for frivolous?

"So we avidly search for our secret truth, only to have appearance teach us who we are?"[2]

*

1. "Les grands moments d'un chanteur."
2. "Dans un miroir."

There we have the key word; but what is truth, here? It is rather a matter of an ineluctable glide toward a truth ever farther in the distance.

Can it be that our actual participation in this movement toward it, however long it may take, is our best chance for reaching it?

". . . how familiar a truth that slips, and in slipping pulls us down as well." [3]

So truth would lie neither at the threshold—where it does not yet know it might be truth—nor at the goal—where it discovers that it no longer is.

"The false certainly contaminated what was true, but the whole took on the color of truth." [4]

Truth cannot claim to be true in general: it can only propose a truth, its own.

Around this proposition, words spin madly, like insects drawn by a lamp.

Everything is touched off in childhood (this vague, undefinable age so much both ahead of and lagging behind its verbal journey, where words speak first of all for themselves, do not speak, are spoken for their own ears alone, lock themselves in their walls, drink their own spittle—as the grown-up "Bavard" will later), and will continue to be touched off by the wonder and bitter disappointment of our first words.

3. Maurice Blanchot: Preface to *Le Bavard*.
4. "Une mémoire démentielle."

So the essential goal is not to convince. What counts is being able to maintain or even widen the field of words in order to allow them to be forever reborn in their daring.

"And if I no longer talked to you? If I refused to listen? "If I no longer saw you?"[5]

Then there would, no doubt, be nothing but an impenetrable absence of universe, a mirror shattered with absence.

"Each deceiving the other and self-deceived."[6]

But is it really a matter of deception?
The "visible field" hides a much larger field of darkness.
Moreover, if the initial aim was to establish a privileged shelter for words—the book?—how could the narrator—the writer—know that this coveted place was and would always be an abyss of silence?

"And more absent for the lack of even a trace of me."[7]
A man who still says "I," but only to state his absence, stands aside for the benefit of a word carried to term, that is, to its ultimate and fatal alienation.

On either side of this word, there crowd in all the words provisionally in circulation. But they never touch it, though they challenge its self-sufficiency and poverty, though they reject the question in favor of a question engendered by this word, but suddenly without interest and automatically ruled out.

5. Ibid.
6. "Dans un miroir."
7. *Les mégères de la mer.*

It is after all possibilities of communication have been exhausted, when the narrator finds himself at this stage of uncommunicability, that he "suddenly has a premonitory vision of what no word could express,"[8] so unbridgeable now the gap between word and thing.

At this extreme point of unlikeness, the mirror reveals only the fleeting image it has caught, image of an image tossed back and forth between the protagonists of a drama—a comedy?—scrupulously performed.

Is the "appearance that would teach us who we are" perhaps only the remembered reflection of a face we are not sure was ever ours, though it claims to be?
Silence is in possession of all the words that, by and by, will break it. Is a word then only a shard we perceive?

But what does all this mean? Is it not the main fuction of speech—of words—to express us? Do we not speak, do we not write, in order to know ourselves?
Appearance, only the *other* can catch hold of. Then who is this *other* through whom we could learn who we are? Is he still, in the infinite of the mirror, we ourselves?
But perhaps the person who speaks or writes is simply an intermediary between word and word, between vocable and vocable, between the image returned by the mirror and his own which he has lost.

But "is it, finally, a question of him?
"Is it he who is in question?"[9]

8. "Une mémoire démentielle."
9. Maurice Blanchot: Preface to *Le Bavard.*

It will never be a question of him because he is sheltered from all questions. He will never be in question because he is, precisely, unequal to asking himself any question. He can only ask it of others, and no sooner done than it no longer concerns him, but the person whose appearance he has assumed.

. . . ask it of others, that is, finally, of the silence that is broken only to re-form out of its innumerable shards.

In the beginning, the white page hides the mirror. Perhaps writing means but working slowly to unveil it. Could this progressive unveiling be its sole object?

Again, an awkward question. To impose an answer would mean a priori to stifle even the smallest impulse to approach oneself directly, in favor of the docile, neutral attitude to which language bids us. As if we had to stand outside language in order to be part of it, to be nothing but language in search of its own constantly deferred truth.

There is always a word to betray the unsayable. Through this betrayal, writing paradoxically regains its dignity.

So what is this "premonitory vision of what no word could express?" Perhaps, simply, a vision of the mirror turned toward the void, toward death, which no more image, no more word, will trouble. Vision of a strange world behind the glass, which escapes the eye, but can be glimpsed—a surprised, transparent reality—in the test and silence of bold thinking as it is engulfed by the sovereign intolerance of the unthought.

Words can only evolve in time. Nothingness is perhaps just a silence that has exhausted all its resources, a silence at the edge of silence, mute, blind, rigid in its space, burned out.

Writing, at this distance, would mean to rekindle, for a moment, the silence.

In the Margins of Yaël
From the Rediscovered Draft of a Letter
to Gabriel Bounoure

In the dark where I am groping, you are present,
ready to throw light.

. . . your letter has been with me constantly. I put off an-
swering to make a series of notes which, it now seems to me,
must be incorporated into the book—provided that the form
of the latter continues not to seem absurd or illusory to me,
or even both. I would then ask your permission to add the
main part of this letter to the "Fore-Speech." It will be my
second letter to Gabriel, the first being in *The Book of Yukel*.

Creation has consecrated God. So God died *after* God, of
His invented death, but also *before* God since He is Creation.

God dies of creating, of creating Himself, dies of perpetu-
ating life by His death: the life of the universe, ours.

Thus we cannot kill God. We can kill only ourselves in God
or, rather, can accept to perish with Him, in each of His acts.

This is why the pages about the crime are not the telling of
a real crime, but the confessions of a potential murderer who
would have assassinated God if that were possible. Avowal of
a madman dogging the tracks—the idea?—of God and the
divine word, a madman who knows himself so guilty in his
heart that he awaits the judge (the police) and will not even
defend himself.

I had, in the beginning, thought of taking some haphazard
crime of passion as a pretext and leading from it to the death
of God, to the death of the writer through the Text.

Have I not always dreamed of writing a book that would continue outside the book, in order, precisely, to get hold of this *outside* where everything is dead before being born, because ready to be born? (For example: Yaël's stillborn child.)

Remains to be seen if it is possible, in the face of the abyss that lies in wait, at the heart of the darkness where it struggles, to make this book . . .

PS. It is not life that creates, but death. Life is created.

"Life is a desperate challenge to eternity, to death."

"Creation creates. *The Creation has consecrated God* would also mean God—Creation—has consecrated—created—God . . ."

In Farewell

It goes its way, certainly. But what is it that has, page after page, participated in this motion: life, death, wounds, desire, thought, questioning, poetry, simple curiosity, confidence, hope?

All of these, clearly, in a reasonable and unreasoned attempt to tackle the written in both its measured calculations and its uncalculable ambition; also in the marvel of an encounter that nothing, in the beginning, allowed us to foresee: the encounter of already saying—which is not what has already been said—with *infinite saying.*

("The wind of the spirit blows only in the desert."

Roger Gilbert-Lecomte)

DATE DUE

JUL 0 8 1993		